THE
Multicultural
LEADER

THE
Multicultural
LEADER

DEVELOPING A
CATHOLIC PERSONALITY

DAN SHEFFIELD

CLEMENTS PUBLISHING
Toronto

Published 2005 by Clements Publishing
6021 Yonge Street, Suite 213
Toronto, Ontario M2M 3W2 Canada
www.clementspublishing.com

Unless otherwise noted, Scripture quotations are from the New International Version of the Bible, copyright ©1973, 1978 by the International Bible Society. Used by permission of Zondervan Publishers.

Cover design and illustrations by Lisa Howden

National Library of Canada Cataloguing in Publication Data

Sheffield, Daniel R., 1960–
    The multicultural leader / Daniel R. Sheffield.

Includes bibliographical references and index.

    ISBN 1-894667-30-1

    1. Church work with minorities. 2. Multiculturalism—Religious aspects—Christianity. I. Title.

BV4468.S44 2005   259'.089   C2003-906457-3

CONTENTS

ACKNOWLEDGEMENTS

Multicultural leaders require shaping through engagement with multiple cultures and interaction with leaders who have gone before them.

I would like to acknowledge the role of my parents, Ron and Dorothy Sheffield, in shaping my early life experience through their engagement with the multiple cultures present in northern Ontario in the 1960s and the openness of their hearts and home to people from around the world over many years.

Likewise a number of friends from different cultures have been influential in helping me see "from the other's point of view." Ken Getty, Carole Guevin, Jon Bonk, Phil and Carmena Capp, Elesinah Chauke, Bongani Hadebe, Harold and Annette LeRoux, Joel and Letty Mayephu, David Yardy and Narendra John, just to name a few.

Dr. Joyce Bellous, education studies professor at McMaster Divinity College, has been an encouraging colleague and friend, creating an environment for collaborative dialogue and philosophical refocusing.

My wife Kathy and our two children, Jamila and Jared. We have travelled the world together enjoying different people, places, cultures, languages and foods. We have learned, been challenged; we have cried with frustration and laughed with joy at our intercultural foibles and triumphs. I appreciate Kathy pushing me toward reality—"what does this mean, how does this work out, in real people's real lives?" I honour Kathy for making the space in our lives for this work.

Dan Sheffield
February 2004
Hamilton, Ontario

INTRODUCTION

The promise of Christian Scripture is that world history is proceeding toward a time when people from every nation, tribe, people and language will stand worshipping together before the throne of God and the risen, sacrificed, Lamb (Rev 7:9,10). This God, who offers love and acceptance through that sacrificed Lamb, desires relationship with all peoples and cultures without negating that acquired cultural identity.

An accepting God, however, is one thing—a community of struggling Christians all seeking after that same recognition and pushing one another out of the way in the process, is quite another. Is it possible that people of different cultures, histories and languages can come together in multicultural communities of faith? Communities expressing acceptance of one another and working together to break down the barriers of differentiation that so easily rear up in front of us?

We should be able to say that, yes, multicultural acceptance is just as possible as the notion that we are dead to our sin and alive to God and therefore able to walk in newness of life with Christ (Rom 6). If God, through Christ, is able to bring change and renewal in this personal dimension of the human condition, surely he desires change and renewal in the dehumanizing, and often violent, interaction of peoples and cultures.

Miroslav Volf in *Exclusion and Embrace* (1996) suggests that it will be the "catholic personality" who will lead us into this new form of intercultural relationship. The broad-minded, generous, inclusive person. These leaders will demonstrate themselves to be a kind of "personal microcosm of the eschatological new creation."[1] They are enriched by otherness; because they have opened up to God's presence at the foot of the cross, they are also open to the different "others" who meet them there.

In this book it is my intention to explore a Christian response to our multi-ethnic urban environments and more specifically to examine the Christian leaders—these catholic personalities—who develop and serve in multi-ethnic congregations.

I will use several terms that are often used interchangeably in popular literature, but which provide a rich understanding when used appropriately. Two root definitions are necessary in understanding terms that are often used in combination with other prefixes. *Ethnicity* is "both a way in which individuals define their personal identity and a type of social stratification that emerges when people form groups based on their real or perceived common origins."[2] In this view, members of ethnic groups believe "that their specific ancestry and culture mark them as different from others."[3] *Culture* is an integrated system of beliefs, values and customs and includes the institutions which express those beliefs, values and customs that bind a society together and give it a sense of identity, dignity and continuity.[4]

Multi-ethnic will be used to refer to groups or settings in which people of diverse ethnic backgrounds are found, where ethnic and cultural difference is a reality. It is a statement of fact about ethnic presence. *Cultural diversity* is an almost synonymous term, but it also identifies broader cultural dimensions of ethnic identity. It is, likewise, a statement of fact about the presence of cultural differences. *Multicultural* will be used in reference to settings that are multi-ethnic in composition and where cultural values are recognized, respected and even embraced, beyond the simple acknowledgement of ethnic/ cultural diversity. This is in contrast to *mono-cultural* settings where one dominant group imposes its values (by intention or by default) despite the presence of persons of diverse ethnic backgrounds. *Multiculturalism* is a socio-political theory that espouses recognition of all cultural communities and the legitimation of their voices in the public arena. An extreme form of multiculturalism seeks *special recognition* of cultural groupings that have been previously, or are presently, disadvantaged, as a means of affirming the identity and self-worth of individuals within that grouping. *Intercultural* is often used to describe a communication or dialogue process between cultural groupings.

In this book I will assert that monocultural and/or multi-ethnic congregations become multicultural, in part, through the development of authentic intercultural communication. This development process is aided by leaders who are able to articulate, embody and practice multicultural self-awareness.

WHY DO THIS WORK?

But why should a Christian congregation want to make this movement from mono-cultural to multicultural, in the first place?

On the first Pentecost of the Christian era, the Holy Spirit filled all those who were gathered in the name of Christ, and they began to speak in other tongues (i.e., distinct languages). In Act 2:5-6 the Jews who were in Jerusalem from the Dispersion "were bewildered, because each one heard them speaking in his own language." Those who heard and experienced this phenomenon serve as a kind of first fruit of the worldwide significance of this event. While most were of Jewish ancestry these Diaspora Jews and proselytes spoke different languages and in many cases reflected different cultural values than their Judean cousins (cf. Acts 6:1-7). New Testament scholar Howard Marshall suggests that this diverse grouping acts as a symbol of the universal need of humanity for the gospel.[5]

The Pentecost event is a vital link in the biblical record of God's concern for all nations—all people groups. Genesis, chapters 10-11 records God's recognition of the diverse families of peoples along with the dispersal of those nations and the confusion of their languages. Throughout the Old Testament God continually challenges the nation of Israel to broaden their view of his universal purposes. This is seen in his special concern for foreigners (Lev 19:33-34), the provision of space in the Temple for foreigners to worship (1 Kgs 8:41-43), and the prophetic vision of Messiah as a light to all the families of the earth (Isa 49:6). Now, Pentecost ushers in the Body of Christ as a new, multi-linguistic, multicultural faith community. Revelation completes the picture of God's "yet-to-be" heavenly kingdom, occupied by groups from all nations, tribes, peoples and tongues (Rev 7:9).

Scripture records God's universal concern, the giving of spiritual resources necessary to realize his intention, and finally a picture of how he sees the ultimate realization of his purposes. This is the foundation of God's multicultural kingdom; the challenge is how the Church will facilitate the development of this multicultural vision.

In Section One we will examine the social theory of multiculturalism in light of a Christian ethical response. Section Two introduces leadership factors which impact upon leaders in multi-ethnic environments and outlines in some detail the capacities required of multicultural leaders. Section Three examines the processes of transformational development which are necessary for leaders who desire to increase their multicultural capacity.

In developing the material for this book I have drawn upon insights from a number of disciplines: social theory, social research methods, biblical studies, Christian social ethics, intercultural communication, leadership studies and education. Several authors who reflect these disciplinary perspectives have emerged as significant in their contributions to my thought processes, in particular: Miroslav Volf, Charles Taylor, Stanley Hauerwas, Eric Law, Charles Foster, Gerald Arbuckle, Stephen Brookfield and Jack Mezirow. In addition, Paul Pearce, a D.Min. graduate from McMaster Divinity College, has contributed research on multicultural churches which was of immense practical help.

It is my desire that this work would be of value to ministry practitioners. Thus, a connecting thread throughout the book is the development of tools and assessment devices that will be useful to multicultural leaders and transferable to congregations that are seeking to develop their multicultural identity. This is not, however, a "how-to" manual for developing multicultural congregations. I would like to suggest this book sets a direction for multicultural leaders to travel; how you get there and what you do there will be your own story, set it your own context. We need authenticity in this journey, not a new one-size-fits-all formula.

Cultural diversity is a state of affairs that we must take into account. It is an accepting and embracing response to cultural difference that leads us toward the multicultural congregation. Therefore, we should concentrate "on fostering the kind of social agents capable of envisioning and creating just, truthful, and peaceful societies, and on shaping a cultural climate in which such agents thrive."[6] This work will seek to give guidelines for fostering multicultural ministry practitioners and for shaping environments in which such practitioners may thrive.

SECTION ONE

A CHRISTIAN VIEW
OF MULTICULTURALISM

CHAPTER 1

IDENTIFYING THE VIEWPOINTS

In the classic 1947 movie *Miracle on 34th Street*, an old man steps up as a substitute for a drunk Santa Claus who was to be the star of New York City's Santa Claus Parade. The premise of the movie is that this old man, appropriately named Kris Kringle, really believes he is Santa Claus and through a few minor miracles and some wise advice convinces many disillusioned people that there really is hope in the world. There is a profoundly moving scene in which a young, homesick and disoriented Dutch war orphan is visiting Macy's department store at Christmas time. When she sees the grandfatherly Kringle sitting in for the drunk Santa Claus she is drawn to the magnetism of the Santa figure. Despite the opinion of her bedraggled and discouraging foster mother that this Santa Claus will not possibly be able to understand her, the hopeful child waits in line to sit on the knee of "Sinter Klaus." When Kris responds to the child in Dutch and proceeds to join her in a Dutch children's song, she is visibly comforted by this act of linguistic and cultural recognition and the foster mother is overwhelmed.

There is in all of us that ultimate desire for personal recognition from a God who would accept us as we are, without condition. Each of us is situated in a culture and society that has shaped and formed our identities; language, history, values and norms which are an integral part of who we are. We have a desire to be accepted as we are-with all of the cultural baggage that accompanies us as we proceed through life.

One of the realities of the North American experience is the diversity of peoples who make up the populations of Canada and the United States. Both countries are the result of mass migration movements over several centuries, overlaid, of course, on the aboriginal cultures already present. Until the turn of the twentieth century, however, most of the immigration to North America was from Europe, which tended to reflect a certain degree of ethnic and cultural homogeneity. The United States has used the metaphor of "the melting pot;" that is, that new peoples must blend in with the predominant values of the culture and assimilate. In contrast, the Canadian context has wrestled with the uniqueness of our two predominant founding cultures—English and French—as well as their interactions with the First Nations and Métis peoples. The expansive geography of the country, in which distinctive groupings of peoples could settle and still maintain their cultural identities with little disturbance, has also contributed to the formation of a unique and diverse consciousness as a nation.

In the modern, urban context, however, the diversity of peoples living in close proximity to one another and still desiring to maintain some level of cultural distinctiveness, has been a challenge. This challenge is not only to civil society and its structures of government, but also to the community of the church. One concern of the Christian community in North America is the threat to the unity of local congregations that is posed by the entry of persons of diverse cultural and ethnic backgrounds, even if they are fellow believers.

How, then, should the Christian community think and act in response to cultural diversity? In this section I will address this question, in part, through introducing the themes of the multiculturalism discourse. The social theory of multiculturalism is discussed as well as several models that Christian congregations have used in response to cultural diversity. I also examine the biblical record in regards to cultural diversity. Does Scripture speak to this issue, or is multiculturalism purely a modern concern? A third area of investigation involves identifying the particular issues at stake from a Christian ethical position. Finally I will seek to discern a course of responsible action for the Christian community on the basis of the material discussed.

MULTICULTURALISM IN SOCIAL THEORY

The Christian community has often struggled with its inability to speak competently to the issues of the day from a Christian worldview. There is a need to communicate in a way that is comprehensible and credible to social theorists and philosophers who have little regard for the Christian voice. Multiculturalism is one of those areas of current philosophic discussion that has received little treatment in the Christian community.[1] Yet it is precisely the Christian community that offers a most striking foundation for the development of multicultural micro-societies. If we are to take this opportunity seriously we must first listen to the social philosophers articulating the issues at stake.

In countries such as Britain, Australia, Canada and the United States, during the last century, we have seen a progression of models that have attempted to create societies with people from diverse cultural backgrounds. The American "melting pot" concept, otherwise known as *assimilation*, assumed that new immigrants would be thrown into the mainstream of American life and would together develop a new amalgam, or uniquely "American culture." In fact, new immigrants were forced for the sake of survival to adopt as quickly as possible the existing way of life.[2]

With the apparent failure of the melting pot, cultural pluralism emerged as the favoured option. Core values and customs of the dominant culture were to be acquired, but ethnic minorities could preserve values and customs—provided, of course, these did not interfere with the core values of the dominant society. However, in effect, the long-term aim remained the same; ethnic minorities must adopt all aspects of the dominant way of life.[3]

In the last quarter of the twentieth century the concept of *multiculturalism* has emerged to express a new and richer dimension in dominant-immigrant culture interaction. In the Canadian context this philosophy has come to be articulated through the metaphor of a "mosaic"—many distinct, individual pieces which combine to make a pleasing whole. Multiculturalism is a social system that purports to offer freedom of choice to those who want to be culturally different in one or more aspects, such as occupation, religious or political beliefs, sexual orientation or ethnic identity. New Zealand missiologist Gerald Arbuckle outlines the foundational assumptions of multiculturalism:

> * That the meeting of different cultures can bring a richness of values to all, including the dominant culture. The stress is on fostering a spirit of positive acceptance, or recognition, of cultural differences.

> * A duality of interaction: adjustment is necessary, on the part of both immigrant and dominant cultures, through a process of positive, dynamic interaction.

> * That only from a position of cultural strength will ethnic minorities be able to move out to contact other cultures with a sense of identity, self-respect and confidence. [4]

In his first assumption, Arbuckle[5] identifies the significance of recognition of difference. An extreme form of multicultural social theory advocates "special recognition"—where it appears to multiculturalism's detractors that different groups are in fact given preferential treatment. Regarding this notion of special recognition, liberal democrats functioning from a postmodern perspective suggest that the dominant culture needs to shift and give space to diversity. This is done within the common vision of civil society, rather than merely letting differences walk alongside the dominant culture.

Arbuckle's point can be explained in greater detail by examining the perspective of social philosopher Charles Taylor.[6] In his essay "The Politics of Recognition," Taylor indicates that

> what we are asked to recognize is the unique identity of this individual or group, their distinctiveness from everyone else. The idea is that it is precisely this distinctness that has been ignored, glossed over, assimilated to a dominant or majority identity. And this assimilation is the cardinal sin against the ideal of authenticity.[7]

Authenticity, or the individual's ability to be true to their full identity, then, becomes a challenge to the notion of universal equality. The principle of universal equality, valued by liberal democracy, suggests that no one should be discriminated against because all have equal rights before the law. In essence, society should be blind to differences between people; each person has individual worth and dignity. Taylor identifies what he refers to as the "politics of difference" by suggesting that this approach "often redefines nondiscrimination as requiring that we make these distinctions the basis of differential treatment."[8] The principle of difference requires that we recognize and even foster particularity. Recognizing particular differences allows individuals to strengthen their identity within the context of their own grouping. Universal equality, it is said, negates identity by forcing people into a homogeneous mold that is untrue to them. Particularity, on the other hand, appears to violate the principle of nondiscrimination.[9]

If we accept the particularity premise of multiculturalism, then what is it that holds a civil society together? Is social cohesion possible if society legitimizes equal recognition of all cultural *groupings*, thus moving beyond the equal worth and dignity of the *individual*? On the other hand, if individuals actualize their humanity and express their unique personalities within the context of differing cultural forms, should not those forms be regarded with equal value as well, not just the individual? In the multiculturalism model, society is challenged to move beyond blindness to difference to, in fact, seeing or recognizing difference.

Professor of religion Steven Rockefeller, when critiquing Taylor's essay on "The Politics of Recognition," states the traditional liberal democratic problem with multiculturalism when he asserts that:

> The democratic way conflicts with any rigid idea of, or abso-lute right to, cultural survival. The democratic way means respect for and openness to all cultures, but it also challenges all cultures to abandon those intellectual and moral values that are inconsistent with the ideals of freedom, equality, and the ongoing cooperative experimental search for truth and well-being.[10]

At this point Taylor affirms that "liberalism is not a possible meeting ground for all cultures, but is the political expression of one range of cultures, and quite incompatible with other ranges."[11] In essence, these writers are suggesting that traditional liberal societies must look for a wider understanding of how to incorporate various worldviews and cultural frameworks within civil society. Multiculturalism is essentially a "commitment to the existence of different legitimate cultural groups as legally sanctioned entities which maintain some separate structures and some structures held in common with all groups in society."[12] In many instances, then, multiculturalism comes into conflict with a traditional liberal democratic view of civil society which tends to support assimilation or limited cultural pluralism.

The reality of many urban contexts is often characterized by processes of "cultural hybridization" in which individuals are continually renovating their values and practices through the encounter with their own culture and the diverse cultures in which they conduct their lives.[13] Popular urban culture can be spoken of "as a present-oriented process of invention through complex hybridizations that cut across class, ethnic and national boundaries."[14] This hybrid mix does not represent assimilation to the dominant culture, nor an acceptance of "bits and pieces" from various cultures (pluralism), but an actual re-creation of a new form of personhood for the multicultural community.

If individual identity and worth is not legitimated within the parameters of the cultural community that has forged that personality, then individuals will feel marginalized and excluded from the dominant culture. In reaction, marginalized groups will feel the need to assert their identity in a manner commensurate to the level of power used in the exclusion process. British educator James Lynch indicates that it is the "the paradox of culturally pluralist societies which wish to pursue democracy, that they must foster cultural diversity to maintain and legitimate social cohesion."[15] This struggle for identity suggests that in a multicultural society difference must be admitted and recognized so that people do not have to strive to make themselves heard, to the detriment of others around them. This perspective "shifts the focus of analysis from cultural preservation to the question of power and its equitable distribution."[16] Recognition of difference does not require preservation of cultural identity, but merely admission that the individual's worldview (however shaped) has a place, a voice, in the conversation.

MULTICULTURALISM AND THE CHURCH

In recent decades, several ways of responding to ethnic diversity have emerged in North American evangelical churches. One method, with a wide number of advocates and practitioners, has been that of the homogeneous, or mono-cultural congregation. The homogeneous congregation emphasizes the development of a particular ethnic, or sub-cultural consciousness as the focus of their outreach vision.[17] Thus a Khmer-language, Cambodian congregation develops as a response to Cambodian immigrants locating in a particular community. This is seen to be the most effective means of reaching this people group for Christian evangelistic purposes. This homogeneous approach would appear to be the dominant model in the church growth movement and carries a lot of weight among church leaders and ministry practitioners. This ministry model responds not only to ethnically diverse communities, but also to other sub-groupings within the dominant culture, such as "Boomers," "GenXers," etc. These groups are all to be treated as mono-cultural targets for effective church ministry development.

A second pattern, that is not so much a model or conscious way of doing things, is that of the mono-cultural, multi-ethnic congregation. In some ways this is the transitional congregation: the church that has been mono-cultural for much of its history and now finds itself in a community undergoing social/cultural transition.[18] This congregation is still maintaining its traditional cultural values, its familiar ways of worship, and "in-group" power sharing. People of diverse backgrounds are essentially expected to assimilate to the existing way of doing things. For those leaders who have developed some conceptual framework for this pattern, it is seen to promote the unity of the faith and the community, rather than breaking the congregation down into special interest groups.

A third model that has emerged more slowly has been that of the heterogeneous, or multicultural, congregation. The heterogeneous congregation emphasizes the enriching aspect of culturally diverse peoples worshipping and interacting together.[19] Thus peoples of Anglo, European, Asian, Caribbean and African backgrounds seek to find ways that affirm, rather than sublimate, their cultural identity in the context of the church which is a community of solidarity—sharing similar beliefs and religious heritage. This is seen to be an affirmation of the gospel message of reconciliation and the concern to break down barriers of separation. Foster indicates that there are several social developments that have contributed to the emergence of the multicultural model of church. The recovery of the experiential in the religious life, the democratization of the sense of self, as well as a tendency to view institutions as serving the individual rather than vice versa, are all factors that influence the life of the multicultural church.[20] In general, multicultural churches tend to have a more holistic view of the connection between the individual and the community of faith—rather than merely as strategic targets, as typified by the church-growth model.

We need to discern a way forward in the dialogue around multiculturalism. Is one of these models more faithful to the biblical record and the fundamental themes of a Christian ethical response? In the next chapter I will examine a number of key biblical passages that reflect God's concern for the inclusion of all peoples, including their cultural identities.

CHAPTER 2

BIBLICAL REFLECTION ON CULTURAL DIVERSITY

Richard Mouw suggests that alongside the divine commandments in Scripture we must place the narratives, the songs, and the eschatological visions:

> From this diversity of materials we learn what God's creating and redeeming purposes are, what sorts of persons and actions the Lord approves of, and so on. Divine commands must be evaluated and interpreted in this larger context.[1]

If we understand ethics as referring to the way we treat other people, then the Christian ethical task "will be one of finding correlations between biblical revelation and moral issues at many different points."[2] How, then, does Scripture treat cultural diversity?

God is concerned with ethnicity, language and cultural differentiation and that concern is evident from Genesis to Revelation. The progressive revelation of God's activity amongst the human race records the interplay between God's judgment upon the nations and his grace that continually points a new way forward to reconciliation. An overview of a selection of biblical passages and themes can introduce some important concepts into this discussion.

THE DESPAIR AND HOPE OF BABEL

The "Table of Nations" in Genesis 10 records the genealogies of Noah's descendants. Already at this point these "families" are identified as distinct "nations," or ethnic people groups, with their own unique languages (10:31). God recognizes their diversity while still desiring to maintain the universal covenant relationship initiated with Noah (9:1-17). As the story ensues, humanity begins to move toward independence from God and his covenant through unification of language (11:1) and effort. They said "let us build ourselves a city and a tower with its top in the heavens, and let us make a name of ourselves, lest we be scattered abroad upon the face of the whole earth"(11:4). When the diverse nations break covenant with God, they identify their need for a forced attempt at unity. They now need an artificial means of unification for fear of being scattered again.

In God's reaction to this declaration he identifies humanity's attempt to seize control, as was attempted by Adam and Eve in the eating of the forbidden fruit. As Blocher points out, "having become a collective enterprise, the sinful project takes on the face of totalitarianism, with technology and ideology as its means of realization."[3] The judgment meted out to this humanitarian experiment is the confusion of languages, "so that they may not understand one another's speech" (11:7). The essence of this judgment is the loss of communication, the breakdown of meaningful relationship because of an inability to communicate. So ethnic and linguistic differentiation, then, is not the result of a normative judgment or curse, nor a divinely orchestrated attempt to keep races and peoples separate. Hauerwas, commenting on this passage, states: "God's confusing the people's languages as well as his scattering of them was meant as a gift. For by being so divided, by having to face the otherness created by separateness of language and place, people were given the resources necessary to recognize their status as creatures."[4] Ethnic and linguistic diversity was already present prior to this judgment; diversity is now enforced as a response to the self-centered desire behind this collective action.

But God did not leave the human community in this isolated position. Even in the Eden judgment, where Adam and Eve learn to deal with the consequences of their disobedience, God's grace provides a way forward toward renewed relationship. So too in the Babel judgment; God does not finish the story with the despair of human separation and alienation. The narrative immediately picks up with the next chapter of God's revelation, the call and blessing of Abraham (Gen 12:1-3). The promise of hope and a future that is given to Abraham and his family is also a promise to all "the families of the earth" (12:3). There is a God, outside of, and therefore not beholding to, any nation, who calls upon one family, one nation, so that he may bless all peoples through his involvement with that one family. The key to attaining this blessing is not through a common human project which requires human effort and communication, but through human-divine communication, the restoration of a covenant relationship. As each people, or family, comes into relationship with God, they meet other peoples already there in conversation with him.

THE NEW COMMUNITY

Ephesians 2:11-22 assures us that God is at work breaking down hostility between himself and humanity, and also between human beings. He is seeking to restore and reclaim his original intention of a human community living in peace, harmony and inter-dependence. This passage is set against the backdrop of the division between Gentiles and God and Gentiles and the Jewish community, as typified by the architecture of the Jerusalem temple. In verse 14 Paul refers to "the dividing wall of hostility."

In the first-century temple constructed by Herod the Great, the temple structure itself, the Court of the Priests and the Court of Israel were all on the same raised level. Descending about 20 steps there was a wall, a stone barricade 1.5 metres tall. Beyond this wall was the Court of the Gentiles, a spacious courtyard from which Gentiles could look up at the temple, but they would not be allowed to approach it.

Posted around this wall were signs, which stated: "No foreigner may enter within the barrier and enclosure around the temple. Anyone caught doing so will have himself to blame for his ensuing death."[5] Paul himself had felt the force of this exclusionary prohibition when he was almost lynched by an angry Jewish mob who thought he had taken a Gentile inside the temple (Acts 21:27-31).

Paul portrays the Gentiles, or all non-Jewish people groups, as "separated from Christ," "alienated from the commonwealth of Israel," "strangers to the covenants of promise," "having no hope," and "without God in the world" (Eph 2:12). This situation leaves the Gentiles—the nations—in complete alienation from God and the Jewish community of faith. But now, those "who were once far off have been brought near"—both to Christ and to the community of faith. The Gentiles are brought near by the work of Christ in his intentional, sacrificial death, his forgiveness of sin and restoration of relationship. The passage states that Christ "is our peace" and it is that tangible peace found in Christ which "makes us both one." It is this intentional act of peacemaking which "has broken down the dividing wall of hostility." Paul suggests, however, that the breaking down of hostility is only the beginning point, the ultimate goal is Christ's desire to "create *in himself* one new humanity" which is only achievable through each individual's personal union with Christ. This new humanity overshadows the Jew-Gentile divide.

In verses 18 and 19 Paul conjures up the image of an oriental court; "through him we both have access in one Spirit to the Father." In the picture Paul draws, many subjects, from diverse backgrounds, are found milling around the courtyard waiting for access to the king.[6] But the picture is altered from a traditional view of an earthly court because all subjects have equal status (the work of Christ) and equal access (the work of the Spirit) to a Father (not a capricious oriental king). There is no longer a need for pushing and shoving, for exclusionary practices, because we all have access to a welcoming Father who makes peace possible amongst his family.

In conclusion, Paul uses three images to describe this new humanity. A *kingdom* in which we are all fellow citizens, a *family* in which we are all members of the household of God, and a *temple* in which we are all inter-dependent "materials" necessary to the building of a spiritual dwelling place for God. It is amongst this new society, amongst his redeemed people scattered throughout the inhabited world, that God takes his place, his home on earth.

THE BODY OF CHRIST

In 1 Corinthians 12, Paul describes the community of Christ-followers as the Body of Christ. Each person in that community is a component in the Body of Christ, a necessary component. The image speaks of each piece of the body having special significance even though it makes a uniquely different contribution. Homogeneity does not work. The body is not made up of similar parts, but of dissimilar ones. Unique components are necessary to the proper functioning of the whole. Precisely because of its diversity of particulars the body as a whole is able to function.

While we understand Paul to be primarily depicting the different spiritual giftings in this passage, he also widens the discussion:

> For just as the body is one and has many members, and all the members of the body, though many, are one body, so it is with Christ. For by one Spirit we were all baptized into one body— Jews or Greeks, slaves or free—and all were made to drink of one Spirit. (12:12-13)

Thus, as Croatian theologian Miroslav Volf has indicated, participating in the Body of Christ "is not a spiritual refuge from pluralizing corporeality."[7] It is not an escape into a universal spiritual space with a homogeneous culture that looks and acts mostly "like I do." It is a space where everyone's unique contribution is necessary and essential to the proper functioning of the whole—a multicultural community of faith giving witness to an accepting God.

ALL PEOPLES AROUND THE THRONE

Finally, Revelation 7:9 paints a picture of a great multitude "from every nation, from all tribes and peoples and tongues" standing before the throne of God, worshipping the Lamb. This phrase records socio-political difference (nations), as well as cultural (tribe), ethnic (peoples) and linguistic (tongues) diversity. The image pulls together the pieces of God's activity in history: the multitude of tongues at Babel is dispersed because of worship inappropriately placed; all the families of the earth are represented in the promise to Abraham. Peoples who were once strangers and aliens to the covenant are now gathered in the presence of God as a multicultural community of faith (Eph 2:11-22). Again this is a heterogeneous picture. This is a God who invites each person, with his or her own personal, cultural, and linguistic identity intact, to come into his presence and take on his character which inevitably discards those aspects of that identity not compatible with a holy God (Rev 21:22-29).

Thus at the conclusion of God's revelation we have a cumulative picture of his acceptance, and desire for the restoration, of all peoples into his presence. In this brief discussion we have identified a number of specific narratives and didactic passages that address the issue at hand. We should, however, go a bit further in identifying themes within the Christian worldview that also speak to the issue of our ethical response to cultural diversity.

CHAPTER 3

IDENTIFYING CHRISTIAN ETHICAL ISSUES

Normative ethics attempts to identify the characteristics of a life worth living, and to examine and articulate standards to inform and guide the shaping of our actions and character. In Christian ethics the primary questions are "What life is worthy of one who recognizes the authority of Christ? What sort of people should those who confess Jesus as Christ be?"

> Christian ethics is the disciplined attempt to explain what the significance of morality is for Christians and to identify those norms that should inform and guide the Christian in his or her way of living towards the world.[1]

Another way of looking at this concern is "how do I understand my identity as one who stands in relationship to God and how do I understand and interact with another whose identity is also related to God?" If God has created both the English-speaking Canadian and the Hausa-speaking Nigerian, and accepted them as part of his family, how is it that I am to think and act responsibly about the interaction of these two diverse persons? Further, how is the collective gathering of the Body of Christ—the church—to think and act responsibly when it conducts its corporate life in a world of cultural diversity?

In Micah 6:8, the prophet asserts that God has shown humanity what is good, acceptable and required: "to act justly and to love mercy and to walk humbly with your God." To merely identify these norms for the Christian life is not enough, however; we need "to elaborate what these norms actually require and how they should be employed in reflection upon the moral lives of Christians."[2] When we look at the issue of cultural diversity and the automatic barriers of difference that are erected, how is it that justice and love can be worked out in the lived experience of the Christian community?

SHALOM

Nicholas Wolterstorff suggests that the biblical, visionary concept of *shalom* communicates best the values of justice, love, mercy, peace and relationship. "Shalom is the human being dwelling in peace in all his or her relationships: with God, with self, with fellows, with nature."[3] Shalom specifically addresses the requirement of right relationships with one's fellow human beings. Shalom is absent when individuals do not make space in their own world for different others. This concern speaks to the issue of justice as well:

> If individuals are not granted what is due them, if their claim on others is not acknowledged by those others, if others do not carry out their obligations to them, then shalom is wounded.[4]

Shalom is not present even if people "do not mind" when their identity is devalued or unrecognized. If the dominant-culture community does not seek to address the devaluing, the lack of recognition of those who are disadvantaged, then justice is missing and shalom is hindered. The community characterized by shalom is ethical, is responsible before God to accept and value the multifaceted existence that he has created. The cultural identity of each individual is acceptable to God and therefore that acceptance and valuation should be translated into the community of faith.

34

IDENTITY AND SELF BEFORE GOD
AND THE WIDER FAMILY

To truly flesh out the meaning of a community living under shalom, we must explore further the issue of relationships. In discussing our response to multiculturalism, how do we understand the transcendence of God over all cultures, while at the same time identifying that he does recognize the individual within his or her own cultural context?

First of all, individuals before God must recognize a change of loyalty. Multicultural leader Stephen Rhodes asserts that "identity based on cultural or racial origin will never be sufficient to make us spiritually mature or whole persons."[5] Suppose the individual is a woman, she is a new creation, someone different than she was without Christ. In one sense she is no longer the woman raised in a rural village in Nigeria, she has become part of the universal family of God. There is a move from the gods of a given culture to the God of all cultures.[6] It is not that she is no longer connected to her culture, but that her primary loyalty is now directed toward the God who transcends culture.

Secondly, though, we can only recognize the liberating universality in Christ, because we come from particular cultural contexts that still impact our worldviews. Paul says we are all one in Christ and then specifically articulates the particularities that are now part of the unified community: Jews, Gentiles, male, female, slave, free—specific recognition of culture, gender and social status. Volf suggests that:

> The body of Christ lives as a complex interplay of differentiated bodies—Jewish and gentile, female and male, slave and free—of those who have partaken of Christ's self-sacrifice. The Pauline move is not from the particularity of the body to the universality of the spirit, but from separated bodies to the community of interrelated bodies—the one body in the Spirit with many discrete members.[7]

In Christ, one leaves behind the sacredness of cultural identity and holds it loosely. Maintaining the proper distance from one's own culture, however, does not remove the Christian from that culture. We are distant from the ideology of our culture and yet we still belong. Volf feels that we should not be moving toward a universal Christian culture,[8] instead there is a need for "a catholic personality, a personal microcosm of the eschatological new creation."[9] This personality he suggests is enriched by otherness; because we have opened up to God's presence, we are also open to other differences. The distance from our own culture that has been created by entering into relationship with Christ does not isolate us but creates space in us for the other. As we are enriched by the experience of difference, so we can enrich the cultures to which we belong.[10]

THE INCARNATIONAL CHURCH

But where is this place where these "catholic personalities" can gather together to be enriched by difference, by the other, who is also in Christ? Hauerwas states that:

> The first task of Christian social ethics . . . is not to make the "world" better or more just, but to help Christian people form their community consistent with their conviction that the story of Christ is a truthful account of our existence.[11]

If the community of Christians, the church, the *ekklesia*, is not a place where gospel values can be lived out in tangible terms where else is it possible?

The social formation of the Christian community, therefore, becomes a primary focus for Christian ethics. There is a need to recover a sense of the church as a collective moral agent. This recovery begins with the recognition of Jesus as a social non-conformist. His meeting with the Samaritan woman, the Syro-Phoenician woman, with sinners, with tax-collectors, all indicate his departure from social and culturally defined norms of interaction. Jesus included the different and the marginalized in the sphere of his relationships—his

Body, the church, can do no less. The church is now the incarnational form of Christ and as such, as John Howard Yoder states, "it is the social reality of representing, in an unwilling world, the Order to come."[12]

The eschatological vision of Revelation 7:9, of all nations and tribes gathered around the throne, must begin to take place in the Body of Christ in this present age. The church community should become a place where people feel safe to reach out and embrace strangers—others—because those strangers have been, first of all, accepted and embraced by Christ. Parker Palmer paints this picture: "the holy city arises in the very process of strangers coming together and bringing the word of life to each other."[13] In fact, Palmer goes on to suggest that "the church could become a kind of halfway house between the comforts of private life and the challenges of diversity—but only if it can stay open to strangeness and help us experience our differences within the context of a common faith"[14]

It is precisely at this point that the issue of multiculturalism in the church encounters reality. Is the church prepared to do the work of being the diverse people of God, the differentiated Body of Christ? Pastor Stephen Rhodes comments, from experience, that Christian leaders will rationalize segregation along homogeneous fault lines;

> they will argue that homogeneous ministry is really the only way out of our decline—that transformational or multilingual ministry is a "wonderful concept" but certainly not practical. They will say that if we are serious about church growth, we should emphasize churches that are homogeneous, not heterogeneous. But clearly this is not what the Bible says.[15]

African-American pastor and community development pioneer, John Perkins provides a sharp critique of both the targeted homogeneous congregation as well as the resistant mono-cultural congregation (as discussed above). He says:

> Today Christians study the science of withdrawing from others and then use it to attract converts. This so-called church growth

or homogeneous principle should make us question the church the same way we question dehumanizing ghettos. It sugarcoats racial separation with a veneer of spirituality and in practice continues the legacy of segregation that divided whites and blacks into separate churches, relationships and agendas.

Homogeneity does not mirror the image of God. It cheapens the people who proclaim it and mocks God's call for us to be agents of reconciliation. What makes it even more harmful is how it is justified: "If we are segregated, more people will come and hear the gospel, which in turn, advances the kingdom of God." This logic spits in the face of a holy God by playing to our human weaknesses and sin nature. At the same time that it increases the size of our churches' membership, it retards our spiritual growth.[16]

In response to cultural diversity, ultimately we have to ask the question: "what would Jesus do?" Would he separate, or would he be inclusive? This is not a theoretical question when in fact we have the testimony of Jesus' life; even in his inner circle were found the different, the marginalized. Christ opened himself to difference and therefore the church must open itself. What remains, then, is for the people of God to more adequately reflect this picture in the practical realities of congregational life. To aid this process we need to go a bit further in defining how the multicultural people of God could and should relate together.

CHAPTER 4

MULTICULTURALISM AND THE CHRISTIAN COMMUNITY

In the present context of globalization, peoples are migrating from hemisphere to hemisphere at an increasing rate. An issue of Canadian magazine, *Maclean's* (December 11, 2000) highlighted the mass immigration from mainland China that is arriving in Canada by illegal means, in steadily increasing numbers. The multi-ethnic world is present with us, particularly in large urban centres.[1] The overlay of cultures in globalizing mega-cities is, in fact, producing "hybrid" personalities and cultures.[2] These are people raised in multi-ethnic communities who actually hold beliefs, values and practices from multiple cultures. They are no longer mono-, or bi-cultural but represent adjusted, re-created, multicultural personalities. The issue before us is how the Christian faith community will respond to this diversity? As discussed above, some churches are maintaining cultural separation as a strategic policy, others are consciously becoming multicultural in orientation, while many struggle someplace in between with changing constituencies, inadequate leadership skills, financial instability and resistant attitudes.

Increasing cultural diversity is the changing reality. But what is God doing in this global transition? Is he putting an opportunity in front of us to demonstrate to the world that his kingdom is the place where all peoples can find common ground while still maintaining their cultural heritage?

AN INCLUSIVE GOD

We have examined in some depth a number of themes, both from biblical study as well as theological reflection that indicate God's desires and intentions regarding the inter-dependence of culturally distinct peoples. We have noted God's particularity in choosing the family and tribe of Abraham to initiate his more universal purposes that all "families" would be drawn into the commonwealth of his inclusive family (Gen 12:3). The "Jewishness" of God's revelation and incarnation was never at the expense of the other nations. And yet that revelation was truly grounded in the identity of the Hebrew people.

We have noted the new community—the new humanity—that was made possible by the sacrifice of Christ, which broke down the dividing walls between God and humanity, as well as between Jews and all the other nations (Eph 2). This new humanity is one in Christ and yet still distinct in its particularities. The image of the Body of Christ, reiterates the value of distinct, unique giftings that contribute to the proper functioning of the whole (1 Cor 12).

John's Revelation gives us the picture at the end of the story, the goal towards which we determinedly move. All peoples, languages, tribes, and nations around the throne. The categories that give us our distinctiveness, clearly spelled out, yet all gathered together for one purpose, to worship the King (Rev 7:9).

Shalom characterizes the desire of God for this world. Peaceful co-existence of all peoples, but not at the expense of justice in which each person's identity and contribution are accepted and validated. And yet those identities are transformed into a new kind of existence as we open ourselves to the entrance of God into our lives. As God enters our lives he brings with him all of those whom he has also transformed, that are now part of our family, and we are called to open ourselves to them as well—to become "catholic personalities."

We have reflected on the nature of the church itself, that space where these transformed people come together before their King, to be fed and blessed by one another and to then go back into their communities with a message of hope and possibility. If the church is not able to demonstrate the incarnational message of Jesus' life and resurrection, then we of all people are most to be pitied.

HOW THEN SHOULD WE CONDUCT OURSELVES?

If the picture that we have painted depicts to some degree the God of Scripture and the Christian community, then how should the church respond to the reality of our multi-ethnic world? Our interpretation should determine our course of action. Do the dominant values of a particular national culture need to be held as sacrosanct in the context of the gathered, multi-ethnic Body of Christ? Do we maintain our separate worlds and affirm mono-culturalism in an ethnically diverse community? Or, do we rise to the challenge of multiculturalism where differing ways of perceiving the world are recognized and validated, and where cultural heritage is accepted as is ethnicity?

In the evangelical community there has been recent debate on the issue of tolerating and accommodating cultural difference.[3] Canadian author Don Posterski, however, suggests a third way between intolerance and acquiescence, what he calls *collaboration*. Posterski says "collaborators are concerned for tolerance too, but in a more moderate way. They contend that we must make room for new expressions of diversity, but they also set limits on the forms of cultural diversity we collectively embrace."[4] His third option connects with Charles Taylor's concern for authenticity. Posterski suggests that "resisting permissiveness encourages us to establish personal convictions and thereby be true to *ourselves*. Relinquishing the right to judge others who are different from ourselves gives other people room to be true to *themselves*."[5]

It is my conclusion that the Christian church should function within the basic convictions of multiculturalism. It is a given, however, that all cultures, including the dominant Western culture, are prepared to submit their values to the examination, sifting and transformation of Scripture. As Rhodes suggests: "the multicultural church, although not demeaning or negating culture, does call us to a transcendent identity in Christ, as well as a transformational citizenship that lies in the reign of God."[6]

Therefore we assert that the meeting of different cultures in the context of the community of faith can bring a richness of values to all as we foster a spirit of positive acceptance of cultural differences. We must submit ourselves to a duality of interaction; i.e., both the dominant and the diverse cultures must be open to positive adjustment through a process of dynamic interaction. It is only from a position of cultural confidence, attained through self-respect, acceptance and validation, that ethnic minorities will be able to interact positively with other cultures. As Hauerwas and Willimon state: "the church is the one political entity in our culture that is global, transnational, transcultural . . . and the tribalism of nations occurs most viciously in the absence of a church able to say and to show, in its life together, that God, not the nations, rules the world."[7]

CONCLUSION

The implications of "Christian multiculturalism" are far-reaching. The move toward a demonstration of the multicultural, heterogeneous character of the Body of Christ will only happen as individual Christians, guided by the vision of a multicultural God, and given permission by their spiritual leaders, are ready to receive the other—the stranger—into oneself and to undertake "a readjustment of identity." [8]As we reach out and embrace the different one, we must make a place within ourselves for difference, while still remaining true to our own God-given identity. As we make a place within ourselves for difference, then our community of faith begins to take on a different texture as well. We are no longer just individuals but members of a Kingdom community which is beginning to welcome the different other (see Figure 1).

It is from this context, then, that we begin to examine what the multicultural congregation looks like, and in particular, the leaders who develop and shape such congregations. What kind of leader recognizes, accepts and welcomes cultural diversity? And, how are such leaders to be developed in the life of a congregation?

A Multicultural Kingdom Identity

Figure 1 — [Daniel R. Sheffield]

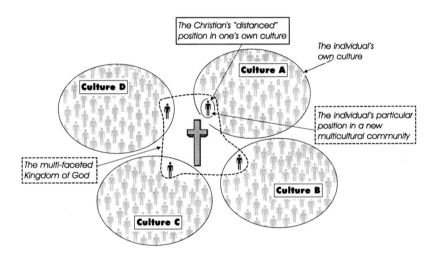

Figure 1: All of us are rooted in different cultures and worldviews. The small stick figures represent Christians who are moving from loyalty to our own cultural values, to an adjusted worldview as a result of our new kingdom identity. We have loyalty to Christ and are seeking to incarnate him as "counter-" in our own cultural contexts, but we also seek to interact and adjust to believers of other cultures. The kingdom identity portrays a new, diverse, non-uniform community of believers from various cultures with adjusted worldviews, looking to Christ as our centre. We become part of this multicultural community while continuing to be impacted by our own cultural identities.

SECTION TWO

DEFINING THE
MULTICULTURAL LEADER

CHAPTER 5

THE CHARACTER OF
OF A MULTICULTURAL LEADER

When we think of the church we must conjure up a picture not of people like ourselves, but of people of all colours and shapes and ages, women and men speaking different tongues, following different customs, practicing different habits, but all worshipping the same Lord... that is the church that Jesus sees.
—S.D. Gaede

My first conscious encounter with cultural difference—the beginning of my own multicultural self-awareness—came when I was in Grade Four. I was attending a public school in northern Canada. I was already aware that when playing in the homes of school friends I was likely to hear other languages and taste different foods than in my own home. We lived amongst people who were first generation immigrants from Finland, Italy, Great Britain, Ukraine and Czechoslovakia. On this particular occasion, however, I was at school and we were singing an action song that required all the students to hold hands. Sally was a black-haired, dark-skinned girl ("a native") who always wore raggedy clothes. No one was willing to hold her hand. After all the students had passed her along the line, it was left to me. I remember making a conscious decision to reach out my hand toward her. I took her hand. I remember it being a bit rougher feeling than the other girls' hands but otherwise, no difference. In one moment, race, class and gender barriers were crossed. For a nine-year-old boy the gender chasm may have actually been the greater barrier!

This moment of acceptance had its roots in the previous summer. My parents spent three weeks conducting Vacation Bible School programmes on three different Indian reserves in northern Ontario, with four kids in a tent trailer. In our family, as I grew up, race and culture were often subjects of discussion but never of derision. We were taught, and had modeled for us, the truth that God loves people of all cultures and our lives should be a testimony to his compassion for all peoples.

Congregations which exist in culturally diverse communities have two options before them. They can interact with the community as mono-cultural organizations serving in a multi-ethnic context, or they can embrace the basic convictions of multiculturalism.[1] *The multicultural Christian community* acts with respect in regard to cultural difference. It accepts the need for members of both dominant and minority cultures to be open to adjustment through personal interaction. In addition, such communities recognize the need for intercultural dialogue in which people of diverse ethnic backgrounds maintain a sense of cultural identity as a means of validating their voice—their uniqueness. These multicultural congregations desire to be a place where the vision of an inclusive God can be lived out in practical reality to the best of their God-given understanding and ability.

Christian congregations, functioning in multi-ethnic environments, which embrace the diversity of cultures in the spirit of an inclusive God, thereby become multicultural congregations. But what are the requirements for leadership in such faith communities? What self-awareness concerning multicultural interaction is necessary in such leaders?

This section reviews leadership models presented in business and educational literature. Also discussed are models of leadership in the unique environment of the Christian faith community. In particular, Christian leadership models suggested by multicultural practitioners are examined. These perspectives aid in building a profile of multicultural leaders, by outlining the cognitive processes, attitudes, skills and practices necessary for the development and on-going maintenance of multicultural congregations.

"Leaders" are those persons who have oversight of the policies and practices which develop and sustain the vision and goals of a local congregation. This includes both pastoral leaders and the elected and informal leaders who take on this responsibility. Leaders in multicultural congregations need to reflect an awareness of their role that is rooted in a view of God as one who welcomes all persons, regardless of their cultural frameworks. This perspective is developed through personal intercultural experience, theological reflection and intentional skill acquisition.

A typical definition of leadership suggests these are people with "the capacity to influence the thoughts, behaviours and/or feelings of others."[2] "Capacity" can refer to an *ability* to influence, but it also implies the notion of substance or volume as in a collection of attitudes, abilities and skills. I will use this collective sense when discussing a leader's *capacity* to influence. Influencing can involve both direct means (e.g., teaching, group skills) as well as indirect means (e.g., attitudes, personal relations). Both direct and indirect means are necessary to stimulate leaders, at all levels of their being (cognitive, affective, physical), to achieve developmental goals.

There are several leadership approaches that will be discussed and a variety of terms are employed that reflect both direct and indirect means of influencing people. *Envisioning* refers to the leader's ability to see and communicate a clear picture of a possible future. *Embedding* refers to the means by which leaders firmly fix the values and practices that they perceive are appropriate to the organization's goals. *Embodying* refers to the ability of leaders to personally live out the values and practices that they espouse. *Embracing* is understood in the manner articulated by Miroslav Volf and expanded upon by Charles Foster, as that movement of different peoples who desire "to be close to others without losing the integrity of their own identities."[3] *Enabling* refers to the leader's ability to create an environment in which employees or members feel able to take the steps necessary to act upon the values and practices of the organization. *Empowering* refers to the leader's ability to make resources available to employees or members and to encourage them to make autonomous decisions on the basis of those resources.

CHAPTER 6

ENVISIONING THE
ESCHATOLOGICAL REALITY

What is God's picture of how his purposes will work out? The Book of Revelation gives us such a picture. But is that picture just a heavenly one, or should we be developing communities of faith in such a manner that they are fit for that heavenly picture?

Howard Gardner[1] in *Leading Minds: An Anatomy of Leadership* (1995) suggests that leaders relate the stories integral to a community's understanding of its life and mission. Gardner says: "I construe leadership as a transaction that occurs within (and between) the minds of leaders and followers."[2]

TELLING THE STORY

From his research, Gardner outlines several constant features of leadership. The first is "the ability to construct and convincingly communicate a persuasive story."[3] Gardner identifies three types of leaders and the kinds of stories which they tell: visionary, ordinary and innovative. Each of these leadership types has their place in the ongoing development of a community or organization. *Visionary* leaders are rare, only occasionally making their mark on a community. They are distinguished by their capacity to envision bold new possibilities for communities. Gardner identifies figures such as Moses, Jesus, Mohammed, Gandhi, Mother Teresa and Martin Luther King, Jr. as visionary leaders. More common, however, are the *ordinary* leaders who simply relate the traditional story of their group as effectively as possible. These leaders do not really challenge the status quo of their community, but empower members through communicating the identity, values and institutional goals in such a way that forward movement continues. *Innovative* leaders, in contrast to ordinary leaders, take a story that has been latent, or under-used, in the community and give it new attention or a fresh twist. These leaders identify stories and themes in a community's heritage that have been neglected and bring them to the foreground as a resource for the renewal and transformation of the community's life together.[4]

In a sense, leaders in multicultural faith communities will draw from all three of the types of leadership patterns that Gardner describes. Leaders maintain the validity of the life of Jesus Christ as the foundation for the community called the church. There is recognition that modern leaders are only building on the *visionary* work of Christ. They are visionary in the sense that they maintain the biblical vision of Christ's intention for the *ekklesia*. For the most part, Christian leaders are *ordinary*, in the sense that the stories of the Christian tradition are regularly communicated as a means of maintaining the vision, values and goals of the founder. Leaders in multicultural congregations will also need to be *innovative*. There is a need to revive the stories of the Old and New Testaments that depict a God who is seeking after *all* the nations, through the context of one particular culture. There is a need to tell an old, perhaps latent, story of a God who embraces the diversity of his whole creation.

Specifically, regarding the story-telling function, Gardner indicates the difference between addressing a story to a circumscribed, homogeneous group, which has common knowledge and values, and to a diverse, heterogeneous group such as a multicultural community. The heterogeneous group requires a rather simple (not simplistic) story defining sharp contrasts with which all participants can identify.

Over time, as the story begins to be established, the leaders can flesh out a more sophisticated, more multi-dimensional version.[5]

One pastoral leader uses the simple image of a salad to describe the multicultural congregation: "you have all these distinct flavours in the different vegetables that go into the bowl—and they don't lose that flavour through assimilation. But each flavour contributes to the whole. The sum of all the parts—the salad—is better than any of the individual parts by themselves. And the "salad dressing" that ties it all together is Jesus Christ, the Holy Spirit."

Another leader uses an African image of the tree as the focal point of the village which provides shade for the collective activities of the group. "People of different cultures join hand in hand around the tree, which is Jesus Christ, who provides shade and comfort so that the people can sit and talk together about their intercultural challenges. The connection to the tree as the cross is quite obvious; at the foot of the cross we meet others who have also come to find acceptance in Jesus."

AN ALTERNATIVE WORLDVIEW

The Christian community has a particular story of God's redemptive activity through Christ on behalf of fallen humanity. God has chosen to bring about his continuing purposes through the church—that particular group of people who acknowledge the truth of the Christian revelation. Authors Stanley Hauerwas and William Willimon[6] in their book *Resident Aliens* (1989), suggest that "one cannot discuss pastors [leaders] and what they do until one has first discussed the church— which needs these creatures called pastors [leaders]."[7] Hauerwas and Willimon, have expressed their concern about the role of the church in the modern world. Rather than seeking to make the world "more Christian" they suggest the most effective thing the church can do for the world "is the actual creation of a living, breathing, visible community of faith."[8] A dynamic community living out God's intention becomes attractive to the world. The church does not need to accommodate to the shifting whims of what the world "might like" about us today.[9]

Hauerwas and Willimon reflect Gardner's view regarding communicating the story of the organization when they say that "in our worship, we retell and are held accountable to God's story, the adventure story about what God is doing with us in Christ."[10]

Leaders in multicultural congregations often feel a sense of "going against the flow." These congregations are going against the natural human tendency to "tribalize" and function as mono-cultural communities. By struggling consciously with intercultural dialogue, they are also going against the conventional wisdom of the Christian "church growth" industry. Leaders feel isolated within their own denominations where the multicultural congregation is often a minority voice. When congregations choose an alternative to homogeneity, in an intentional manner, there is a need for the story, theology, vision and values to be regularly articulated by leadership.

> *Leaders in multicultural congregations, through personal experience in intercultural settings, and through study of Scripture, reflect theologically on the manner in which the diversity of cultures impacts the nature and life of the church, thus developing a theology of diversity. Multicultural leaders come to see the multicultural congregation as an embryonic form of the heavenly kingdom. These leaders are able to construct and communicate a story of the multicultural congregation that conveys the multi-dimensional, relational character of God, and that redefines the conventional image of the mono-cultural Christian congregation.*

CHAPTER 7

EMBEDDING THE
MULTICULTURAL VISION

Edgar Schein,[1] in *Organizational Culture and Leadership* (1985) describes organizational culture as that grouping of values and practices that shape the character of an organization. To explain his model he uses examples from business firms studied in his research. Schein outlines the processes by which culture is initiated and developed, and the role of leaders in embedding, or fixing culture, and managing culture-change.[2]

On the basis of extensive research in American, as well as multinational, business organizations, Schein discusses the role of the leader, first of all, in starting companies and embedding values and practices into an organizational culture. Schein describes the leader's role in embedding values in the operative culture of an organization through various mechanisms. Some of these embedding mechanisms are conscious, deliberate actions, while others are unconscious and may be unintended.[3] From his research, Schein outlines five "culture-embedding" mechanisms that shape an organization. He identifies these as the following:

1) what leaders pay attention to and control;
2) how leaders react to critical incidents and crises;

3) deliberate role modeling and coaching;

4) criteria for allocation of rewards and status;

5) criteria for leadership selection and recruitment[4]

In summarizing his thoughts on culture-embedding Schein notes that: "a dynamic analysis of organizational culture makes it clear that leadership is intertwined with culture formation, evolution, transformation, and destruction."[5]

REDEFINING ORGANIZATIONAL CULTURE

In discussing the management of culture-change, Schein suggests that "the unique and essential function of leadership is the manipulation of culture."[6] By manipulation Schein understands the means, both direct and indirect, by which a leader embeds particular values and practices in an organization. Leaders need to be able to articulate their own assumptions and values in a clear manner and "to embed them gradually and consistently into the mission, goals, structures and working procedures of the group."[7] In managing change in organizational culture Schein speaks of "cognitive redefinition," that is, reorganizing the manner in which people think about, or understand, their beliefs, goals and actions.[8] If an existing organization requires significant change to continue to meet its present mission, or to move towards a new *raison d'etre*, leadership must have the ability to induce this redefinition by communicating and winning support for new visions and concepts.

It is not just the formal leadership, however, who will take change forward. Schein draws upon his own research in process consultation and group dynamics when he says leaders "must recognize that in the end, cognitive redefinition must occur inside the heads of many members of the organization and that will happen only if they are actively involved in the process."[9]

In conclusion, Schein wonders about the leadership development process:

> If leadership is culture management, do we develop in our leaders the emotional strength, depth of vision and capacity for self-insight and objectivity that are necessary for culture to be managed?[10]

Schein's means for *embedding culture* are of particular interest for leaders in multicultural congregations. The vision of a multicultural faith community goes against the conventional wisdom of many evangelical denominations. The "church-growth," homogeneous model has been accepted for so long that other ways of conceiving the church have become almost heretical. Leaders need to be confident about the "rightness" of their approach, as well as having the ability to clearly articulate both theory and practice—so as to "embed," through practical mechanisms, a multicultural culture: a new way of seeing, being and doing church.

A pastor with experience in multicultural ministry had several conversations about the relative values of homogeneous and heterogeneous congregations with a denominational leader responsible for church growth and church planting. This leader was well-versed in homogeneous church planting and had seen significant success in this method and was very skeptical of a multicultural model. He had, however, had very limited intercultural experience and little understanding of how to listen to the voices and expressions of other cultures. This leader, subsequently, was able to participate in a cross-cultural research assignment in an Asian country. In that process he realized that many of his notions of ministry competence had to take a back seat to the competence of Asian leaders, whom he had previously dismissed and regarded as "out of step" with "modern (North American) methods." It was this required adjustment (cognitive redefinition) to other ways of seeing ministry competence which ultimately led this leader to an acceptance of the multicultural model, in which all cultural voices are empowered to contribute to decision-making.

CULTURE-CHANGE

Managing culture-change, as Schein has outlined, is a significant skill since many leaders are faced with the need to move toward the multicultural model just to survive. As urban areas learn to deal with the reality of changing demographics, existing mono-cultural congregations inevitably become multi-ethnic or they eventually close their doors. Existing congregations have to go through a redefinition of their identity, vision and goals to begin to function multiculturally. The wise leader will manage this "culture-change" through a group consultation process so as to bring as many people into the new configuration as possible.

One pastor, seeking to develop multicultural adjustment in his congregation, instituted a number of inclusive practices over several years. These practices seemed "good at the time" to his essentially mono-cultural, Anglo leadership team; they agreed to the changes. However, over time, these practices began to grate on the comfort zone of many of the leadership team. Eventually this led to the departure of the pastor. As the congregation began searching for a new pastor they went through a process of examining their needs, concerns and future intentions. They were presented with two pastoral candidates, one who fit perfectly their past paradigm and one who was even more multiculturally-oriented than the pastor who had just left. They chose the pastor with "the catholic personality." The leadership team realized that culture-change had happened; "cognitive redefinition" had taken place; they were no longer thinking and acting in a mono-cultural mode. Their future lay in a leader who would continue to draw all the cultural voices into the decision-making processes of the congregation, to embed the multicultural vision.

Schein's concluding question about leadership development is equally valid for the multicultural congregation. Are we developing leaders with emotional and spiritual strength who have a clearly articulated theology and vision, the capacity for reflection and a willingness to work communally? These are the necessary attributes of leaders who want to develop multicultural faith communities.

Leaders in multicultural congregations must be able to communicate this story/vision in a manner that draws others into the process through a redefinition of group identity and dynamics and a distribution of power in an equitable manner that allows all to have a sense of ownership. It is this communication and alteration that will embed the vision in both a cognitive and relational manner.

CHAPTER 8

EMBODYING MULTICULTURAL RELATIONSHIPS

One of Gardner's features of leadership is "the capacity to embody the story in one's own life."[1] Crucial to the telling of a particular story is whether the leader "embodies" the story, "whether the leader's own actions and way of life reinforce the themes of a story that he or she relates."[2] And, as in Schein's model, this story must be lived out in the personal relationships of the leaders, not just communicated in a cognitive, disconnected manner. Leaders must embody the Christian story.

Living in urban South Africa in the late 1990s was not the place to be if your skin was white. The city centres of South African cities, traditionally "whites-only areas," began emptying of whites even before the majority black government came to power in 1994. Crime, violence, domestic abuse, rape and alcoholism were becoming characteristic of the city centres. Likewise the city centres were becoming the most culturally diverse locations in South African society. People of all cultures, languages and people groups were moving into the city centres. Our assignment was to plant a multicultural congregation in this setting. So we moved our family, with two young children, into the multi-ethnic city centre of Pietermaritzburg, capital of KwaZulu-Natal province.

One evening, some months after our arrival, the music from the multi-family house next door was so loud that sleep was impossible; I decided to join the crowd. The alcohol was flowing and the Rasta man was wailing out Bob Marley songs as I brought over our worship team's African conga drum. After several hours the music faded and the mood got mellower. Michael, one of our colourful neighbours (in Afrikaans, a *skelm,* or mischievous petty criminal), asked me a question. He used the respectful Zulu term for pastor; "*Mfundisi,* why are you living here? Everyone else has moved out of this place, we can't understand why you have come here." The next day he came over and asked me to help him unplug the fouled toilet that was overflowing throughout his house. I did.

Eric Law, a Chinese-American minister[3], in his book *The Wolf Shall Dwell with the Lamb: A Spirituality for Leadership in a Multicultural Community* (1993), takes a deeper look at culture and power and the practical translation of intercultural dialogue into personal relationships.

Law draws a connection between the skill of power discernment and the need for a deeper understanding of the significance of the death and resurrection of Christ. Those who have a sense of their own personal power must come to a place of disempowerment before the cross. This is the place where we also meet our brother or sister of another culture. There is no room for a power imbalance at the foot of the cross. Likewise those who lack a sense of personal power must recognize their empowerment in Christ in light of the resurrection. Law states that "the gospel commands the powerful to give up power and the powerless to endure and be faithful. Furthermore, the Gospel story empowers the powerless to take up the power to do the mighty works of God."[4] Multicultural leaders need to act out (embody) a spirituality rooted in the Gospel story.

Pastors often have a need to be needed! In many cultures the role of a pastor or spiritual leader is highly respected, further enhancing a pastor's sense of his own self-worth. Leaders in multi-ethnic congregations could tend to profit from this respect. The role of pastor-equipper found in Ephesians 4, however, requires less of a "commander" and more of an "empowerer." The difference between a multi-ethnic church and a multicultural congregation can be reflected in the manner in which their leaders either accept cultural deference to their authority/power or lay that deference down and encourage/empower the voices of the disempowered. This "laying down" is a challenging spiritual act as well as a skill required of the multicultural leader.

Law focuses on the nature of intercultural dialogue and the need to acquire skill and practices that enable the creation of an environment where all participants experience a sense of equality and the ability to express themselves wholly. The exercise of these inclusive, interpersonal skills flows from a spirituality rooted in the character of an inclusive, accepting God. Together these skills and inclusive spirituality allow the leader ministering in a multi-ethnic environment to embody the worldview which they espouse.

Leaders in multicultural congregations must give up their leadership "power," their "expert status," and develop a spirituality rooted in servanthood. Genuine, authentic, relational dialogue across cultures, as a way of life, is required to embed the multicultural vision in an experiential, affective manner in the heart and soul of the congregation. The manner in which leaders conduct themselves interculturally will have direct correspondence to congregational life.

CHAPTER 9

EMBRACING CULTURAL DIVERSITY

In his book *Embracing Diversity: Leadership in Multicultural Congregations* (1997), Charles Foster[1] reflects on his research with three multicultural congregations in Atlanta, Georgia. He suggests that leadership in such congregations must be transformative, anticipatory and relational. These adjectives describe the manner in which the vision of a different kind of faith community is worked out by its leaders.

Regarding *transformative* leadership, Foster says leaders must nurture change because maintenance is not an option. He comments that in the congregations in his study, transition to a multicultural congregation began with the arrival of a new pastor with an ability to reinterpret congregational values and focus on previously latent biblical images. A new pastor, with a new vision, is not enough however. An eschatological vision of acceptance and equality has to be translated into the practical redistribution of power in a more inclusive manner.[2] The new vision only takes root as people begin to hear and respond to new possibilities for their congregation in the stories being articulated. Transformation occurs when hesitant people catch the vision of the pastor and stay with the congregation "through the struggle to re-envision itself."[3] The new vision must be powerful enough "to sustain the congregation through the fears experienced in the midst of often radical changes."[4] This ability "to embrace the fear of change is a major feature in the pastoral and lay leadership of multicultural congregations."[5]

In this transformative process, leaders must have the ability to facilitate "mutual critique."[6] In Foster's words, mutual critique "requires that members of each racial and cultural group grant the others 'sufficient respect' to listen, and trust enough to challenge and critique" one another.[7] In emerging multicultural congregations it is often a long process to move beyond being preoccupied with hurting each other's feelings, to a reciprocal candor about expectations and responsibilities, in order to discuss moral and theological strengths and blind spots.[8] As Foster indicates:

> Mutual critique ... involves more than a rational intellectual assessment and prioritizing of another's ideas, practices, and moral perspectives to ensure fairness, equity, and justice in con-gregational life. It culminates in the intensification of the spiritual ties binding one person to another, one group to another.[9]

Each individual and each cultural community must come to recognize itself in the loving critique of the other as well as give and receive forgiveness where hurt and misunderstanding has occurred.

Glen Kehrein and Rollie Washington, white and black ministry leaders at Church of the Solid Rock in Chicago describe "fudge-ripple meetings" at their church. Once a quarter, the black and white members of their congregation meet in separate caucus groups to discuss irritations and problems with each other. The black caucus identifies all the issues that they feel are results of racism and non-inclusive practices on the part of white church members. The white caucus discusses all the problems that they encounter in the values and practices of the black church members. Then each group appoints a spokesperson to articulate their concerns in a joint session of the two groups. Discussion is held until issues are resolved or steps forward are identified. The leadership team has found that having a regular, intentional, critique (griping) session allows legitimate concerns to be stated freely and clearly, rather than allowing issues to fester unspoken or contribute to gossip or backstabbing.[10]

In Foster's view, *anticipatory* leadership is proactive in regard to questions, issues and problems that naturally arise in the multicultural congregation. Leaders must reflect and prepare for possible responses. Situations or events must be seen from a future perspective—the point of destination. The memory of the community's future vision has priority over the memory of its history. For leaders in multicultural congregations there are few precedents to guide their efforts. There are few details on how to achieve their goals and few have any experience of building multicultural communities. It is the possibility of a new reality that carries them forward.[11]

When Foster talks about *relational* leadership he highlights the need for intercultural dialogue. Feminist ethicist, Sharon Welch challenges the notion of multicultural harmony when she says "the idea that there is a common interest, shared by all, reached by transcending our special interests, is fundamentally ideological."[12] This is an important critique of the multicultural vision because ideology is often divisive. Whose view of multiculturalism do we take? The white/privileged view, or the coloured/disempowered view? Therefore intercultural dialogue must take precedence over a "multicultural ideology", so that an authentic process happens. Existing institutional structures, including the church, "perpetuate oppressive, paternalistic patterns of relating," therefore people-oriented, relational, "open-minded engagement with structures and power realities" is necessary.[13]

Further, Foster suggests that in intercultural dialogue "empathy" (as traditionally understood) is almost impossible; can one really understand or share the perceptions, thoughts or feelings of the different other? Can men really understand the impact of childbirth upon women? Can the rich really understand the poor? The differences in background and perceptions are too deep and profound to be shared. Therefore congregational members must engage in what Foster refers to as "a suspension of expectations."[14] Cultural assumptions and perspectives are *suspended*, allowing people to enter into the other's world of assumptions, beliefs and values, and temporarily taking them as their own.[15] They must see, value and feel as the other sees, values and feels. Relational leaders facilitate processes where this suspension can occur.

An earnest, young Christian couple were trying to help a group of Central African refugees to start a church in a Canadian city. In describing their reasons for abandoning the project the couple clearly articulated their unrealized expectations regarding worship style and "starting on time." They complained about people "shouting and hollering," about people "praying all at the same time," about children running in and out of the worship area. They referred to certain group leaders as "liars" because they "never kept their word, they would never show up on time." The only good thing about the church was the Sunday School because the Canadian couple taught it and could depend on themselves to show up and get the work done; they even "had those kids sitting still and minding their manners."

This true story illustrates what it means to *not* suspend cultural expectations! This couple were lacking someone to help them suspend their own ethnocentric expectations and to enter into the world of Central African Christians. A world where clocks and watches have no meaning; where a worship service is a celebratory event—an escape from the hopelessness of the refugee existence in a camp made up of thousands of tents, far from their homeland. A world where loud, insistent prayer is a way of pouring out aching hearts before a listening God. A world where keeping one's word is not the difference between 8 and 9 o'clock. This couple needed to "see from the other's point of view" and let those observations adjust their own expectations.

In conclusion we observe that Foster's comments on *transformative* leadership resonate with the issues raised by Gardner and Hauerwas and Willimon. Leaders in multicultural congregations need the ability to articulate a fresh or renewed vision of future possibilities.

Foster and Welch's insights on *relational* leadership highlight the unique component of intercultural dialogue in the multicultural congregation, which is so dependent upon interpersonal capacity— both the desire and the ability to relate inter-culturally.

> *Leaders in multicultural congregations know that they continually need to understand more about intercultural dialogue. They know they need to move from "ethnocentrism" in their worldview to "ethno-relativism"— to hear the other fully without passing judgment. They know they need to develop a body of knowledge regarding how different ethnic groups think, act, and feel in different contexts. They know they need to understand and assess power dynamics in various groups. They know they need to develop skill in "mutual critique"—hearing and giving constructive criticism about culturally determined values and practices. They need to develop the ability to negotiate shared or mutual meanings. This growing sensitivity demonstrates respect and acceptance in the multicultural congregation.*

CHAPTER 10

ENABLING INTERCULTURAL EMPOWERMENT

I n the evangelical stream of the North American church there has been great emphasis on the "church growth" model of leadership style. In this approach leaders of growing churches are often seen as more *project-* than *people-*oriented, more *goal-* than *relationship-*oriented, more *authoritarian-* than team-oriented. This is often referred to as the "guru" management style. Christian Schwarz,[1] author of *Natural Church Development* (1996) suggests, however, there may be confusion between the descriptions of "large" and "growing" in this guru model. Schwarz indicates that it is in fact large churches that work well with this leadership model, but it does not necessarily mean that growth is happening.[2]

In his book, Schwarz raises the concern about a focus on quantity rather than quality. Focus on quantity often means that aspects of the communal life of the congregation suffer in the name of growth. His research was based upon extensive surveys conducted with an international range of churches that were either growing or declining. In light of his research, Schwarz concludes that churches which maintain healthy corporate life are more "effective" in new conversion growth, than churches which give all their attention to "growth strategies."[3] In essence, the internally healthy church is more attractive than the church that devotes a disproportionate amount of its energy, time and resources to outward orientation.

From his research, Schwarz found that quantitative-oriented and qualitative-oriented leaders conduct themselves and their ministries in more or less similar terms with regards to goal-orientation and people-orientation. Where there was the most significant difference in ministry practice was in the qualitative leaders' concern for "empowerment;" i.e., "the leader assists Christians to attain the spiritual potential God has for them."[4] The quantitative leaders tend to use lay workers to help the pastor or the institution achieve their goals; the qualitative leaders "equip, support, motivate, and mentor individuals, enabling them to be all that God wants them to be."[5] Gardner concurs when he suggests that competent leaders need to increasingly utilize empowered followers— "the leader does not need to be an expert on all the details."[6]

Schwarz concludes that this empowerment model of leadership requires a spiritual self-organization: leaders must recognize their place in a system that acknowledges God as the energy behind the community, rather than human effort and pressure. Leaders realize their own empowerment as they empower others through discipleship and delegation—they no longer have to handle the weight of church responsibilities on their own.[7] Empowering leadership also implies giving up "the expert" role with its attendant power and status in the faith community, which can be a frightening, but ultimately redemptive, act in itself. In empowering, responsibility and power is distributed more equitably.

The multicultural congregation, in particular, requires that power be de-centralized, so that all those sitting around the table are recognized as having a valid voice, equal in value and worth to the community as a whole. This empowering model, in a sense, gives away power from "the expert" or "the core group" to multiple leaders, through the equipping and discipling process. Every person has a role to play in maintaining the health of the diverse community.

Ultimately the multicultural congregation will rise or fall based upon the sense of belonging and ownership that each participant experiences. In general, ownership is attained through empowered involvement.

The multicultural leader must discover appropriate means for enabling intercultural empowerment—so that inclusive practices are led by confident, equipped leaders. More than "diversity" or "multiculturalism" the term "intercultural" signals action and interaction, exchange and integration of difference into one's everyday institutional life. "Intercultural relations" defines the ways in which people lay their differences on the table as a matter of course and work, communicate, coalesce across those differences in order to understand and be understood. Empowerment is about the process by which people learn from new information, new ways of thinking, and begin to act confidently upon those insights.

A pastor had the following conversation with an older Korean gentleman in his congregation.

"Mr. Kim, we all call you "Mr. Kim" at our church. What do you like to be called?"

"You may call me Mr. Kim if you wish, that is fine. My full name is Yong-Sik Kim. There is no such thing as a middle name in Korea, just a first name and a surname. "Kim" is my surname. It means "gold" or "iron" in Korean. "Yong-Sik" is my first name. "Yong" means "roots of a flower" and "Sik" means, "clear water." When I write my name in Korean, I write it Kim Yong-Sik. However, here in Canada, I like to be called "Yong Kim," even in informal settings. To be called just "Yong", in the way that you Canadians greet older people—"Hi Frank!"—would seem somewhat childish. In Korea, only children are called by their first name, and even then, only by other children who are the same age. But to be only referred to as "Mr. Kim" does not give a person the full understanding of my name, my identity."

This dialogue enabled the pastor to gain an appreciation for the meaning of names and proper respect in Korean culture—he will go away with a greater sense of confidence in how to conduct himself with other Koreans and what terms are appropriate. The pastor may even share some of this cultural knowledge with other leadership team members as a means of empowering those leaders in their intercultural encounters with Koreans.

Law further illustrates the intercultural challenge by examining the ways in which different cultures view leadership practices. To talk about leadership as if there are a set of transcendent skills and approaches valid in all cultures, says Law, is deceptive. He feels that "the definition of a leader is not the same in different cultures because how a person is expected to manage a group is dependent on the group members' perceptions of their own power."[8] On one hand, Law describes cultural groups that have a high sense of individual power, where everyone believes she or he is equal to everyone else. In this kind of cultural grouping, the leader enables the group to accomplish its goals through consensus, volunteerism and self-direction. On the other hand, groups with a low sense of individual power will not challenge a leader who is perceived to be an authority figure. In this cultural grouping, the leader is expected to know the gifts, interests and abilities of each member and invite them to take certain responsibilities that will enable the group to achieve its objectives.[9]

When people continue to function from their own perceptions of leadership and group processes, Law calls this "ethnocentrism." As one example, Western background groups may believe that by inviting a person of non-Western background into a committee or study group, they are being inclusive, but they deceive themselves. Law suggests that non-Western people often have a low sense of individual power and place high value on collective action. Those who place a high value on collective action tend to feel isolated and disempowered when functioning in a predominantly Western environment because their strength, typically, is in the group, not the individual. Law suggests, therefore, that leaders need to function in an "ethno-relative" manner. An environment needs to be created "that allows people to interact with equal power and therefore redistributes power evenly."[10] This can be realized, in Law's view, by allowing people with low individual power to caucus regularly, thereby collectively affirming and empowering their voice. This simple practice enables intercultural empowerment; the individual-power group is challenged to allow precious time and space in the schedule and the collective-power group is able to deliberate without social and time pressures. Law indicates that leaders need to be trained to be more culturally sensitive and to do this kind of *power analysis* based upon an increased cultural sensitivity.[11] This adjustment in understanding allows the leader to consciously make choices about his/her personal practices.

In a society that "corrupts and co-opts Christians" into a self-focused worldview, the unique role of the pastor is to help the congregation gather the resources necessary to be "the colony of God's righteousness."[12] If the intentional multicultural congregation represents a responsible form of the Christian community, then pastors need to enable their congregations to think and act in an inclusive manner.

Hauerwas and Willimon suggest that leaders in local congregations "have significance only to the degree that their leadership is appropriate to the needs and goals of the group they lead."[13] The role of the leader in their view is to understand the story of the community and to faithfully communicate that story, with its inherent values and goals, in a manner that will affect the formation of both individual and corporate identity that increasingly reflects the character and purposes of God.

Leaders must find or develop the forms that enable this kind of community to exist. The church that has some degree of success as an intentional multicultural congregation will also have a greater sense of being God's alien people and thereby be more clearly representative of the divine vision seen in Revelation 7:9.

Leaders in multicultural congregations are intentionally seeking out skills that will enable and empower the multicultural vision to take root in an increasingly practical manner. They know that creating an environment where everyone is able to interact with equal standing, assured that they are being heard, requires specific skills in intercultural group dynamics. They need to find or develop their own forms of interaction that will enable the alternative community to come into being—forms that suspend cultural expectations long enough for meaningful understanding to happen. They need to develop skills in group dialogue processes where individuals can undergo "a readjustment in identity"—in order to draw closer to Christ and to one another, rather than to a particular cultural perspective. This toolbox of intercultural skills will be used on a regular basis and is necessary to the free dialogue required by the multicultural community.

LEADERS FOR THE ROAD LESS TRAVELLED

The multicultural congregation is a unique community in a world that constantly chooses the easiest, least vulnerable path through inter-cultural, interpersonal relations. To have a role in the leadership of a community that takes the hard way requires a particular set of attitudes, values and skills. Volf speaks of "the catholic personality," a kind of first-fruit of the eschatological new creation, the new community that Christ ushered into the realm of human existence.[14] People with this broad, inclusive outlook are fundamental to the growth and development of multicultural congregations. In this chapter a number of models of leadership practice have been discussed and inform the profile presented.

At the outset I suggested that leaders are people with the capacity to influence the thoughts, values, behaviours and/or feelings of others. The capacity to influence can refer to a collection of attitudes, abilities and skills, rather than just a simple ability. In building the *Multicultural Leader Profile* I have drawn from various sources that are rooted in the best practice of a whole body of leadership approaches and have sought to integrate these insights into a useful assessment tool.

From Schein we have borrowed the notions of "culture-embedding" and "cognitive redefinition." From Gardner we have borrowed the importance of articulating a particular story that motivates a community, and the necessity of "embodying" that story in the life of the community. Schwarz alerts us to the importance of "empowering" leaders and building "ownership" amongst the congregation. Hauerwas and Willimon confirm the importance of communicating a visionary story rooted in the counter-cultural nature of the Christian message, a story that "enables" the alternative faith community to grow and flourish. Foster raises the concern for authentic dialogue, for mutual critique, and for the need to move forward through the fear and disappointment of change and transition, in order to "embrace" difference. Law emphasizes the importance of intercultural dialogue as well, but suggests the need for particular skills in "ethno-relativism" and "power analysis." Law also raises the concern for a spirituality that reflects the incarnational nature of Christ's life, death and resurrection in which we take Christ's example of voluntarily giving up power and privilege for the sake of God's kingdom.

In both Foster and Law, as well as from the best practice of other multicultural leaders, great importance is attached to the need to develop skill in inter-cultural dialogue—to develop multicultural capacity. At the same time the more cognitive approaches of Schein and Gardner serve as the foundation upon which the ministry practices are built. What ties the two orientations together, as reflected particularly in Law and Hauerwas and Willimon, is a spirituality rooted in the cross and the resurrection—the incarnational life and ministry of Jesus Christ, and a personal disposition to listen and accept the different one.

Taken together, we can apply these leadership approaches to the development of multicultural leaders. I suggest that it is these attributes which define the multicultural capacities required of leaders serving in multi-ethnic congregations. The characteristics are really collective categories that have numerous implications for practice. At the same time the characteristics are specific enough that assessment processes can be developed which would be precise and measurable.

If the dividing wall of culture and difference has been broken down by the sacrifice of Christ (Eph 2:14-16) then the notion of the multicultural congregation must be possible. This new reconciled humanity, however, is going to need a new kind of congregational leadership. Leadership which envisions the heavenly reality as already present and possible. Leadership which embeds that possibility into the beliefs and values of congregational life. Leaders who embody the new humanity in their interpersonal, intercultural, relationships. Leadership which wholeheartedly embraces—opens wide to—the "different-ness" of cultural diversity. Leadership which enables all voices to be heard through intentional policies and practices.

MULTICULTURAL LEADER PROFILE

The multicultural leader:
- *envisions the eschatological reality of the multicultural congregation*
- *embeds the multicultural vision in the practices of the congregation*
- *embodies multicultural relationships*
- *embraces cultural diversity*
- *enables intercultural empowerment*

SECTION THREE

BECOMING A MULTICULTURAL LEADER

CHAPTER 11

MEASURING
CULTURAL ADJUSTMENT

A leader in a multicultural congregation must come to understand issues from the other's point of view. In Africa I was asked the question, "when is a person really married in God's eyes?" As a Western Christian I knew the answer to that question—marriage occurs when a man and woman have made a covenant before God in the presence of a minister and other witnesses, and that covenant is legally registered. That is our de facto Western cultural understanding of how marriage is solemnized. When a young person in North America asks a pastor this question we often automatically sense questionable motivation—is this person really asking "can my girlfriend and I have sex if we are in love and know that we plan to marry?" So we give them a very clear answer! But if we think about it there are several pieces to that standard answer that don't stand up to any pattern indicated in Scripture.

In one African culture a marriage process begins when a man expresses an interest in a young woman to his parents or other mediator. His parents approach the woman's parents to assess willingness. If the young woman is favourable to the request then a small earnest payment is given to the parents—as a sign that the man is prepared to back up his invitation to marriage. A bride price is set of perhaps 10 cows or the equivalent in cash, about one year's wages. A date for an engagement party is set, to which the man is obligated to provide a selection of gifts which will be dispersed to the fiance's next of kin. This gift is really the down payment for the woman. Now the young man must begin to pay the bride price. This will normally take many months, even years. When the bride price has been fully paid, then a massive wedding celebration is held. In this culture, however, since a significant down payment has been paid out at the engagement party, it is understood that the man has certain rights to relationship with the woman, even if she does not yet come to live in his home. It is not unusual for children to be born during this interim period while the bridegroom is seeking to pay the final bride price.

When the colonial powers came to this region they declared a marriage to be legal once the final bride price had been paid. The missionaries who came with the colonial powers then established that any sexual intercourse prior to the final payment should be regarded as pre-marital sex; any children as married out of wedlock.

In the present context, however, young Africans, who still follow this same pattern, are asking the question "when is a person really married in God's eyes?" In practice, some Christian young people are going to the justice of the peace to have their marriage solemnized in a civil arrangement in advance of the full bride price being paid. In a depressed economy it can take years for the man to earn enough cash to meet the criteria. So to circumvent the traditional practices adhered to by their parents and the church, they take matters into their own hands. When they finally have the bride price paid off then a full celebration and church wedding is held.

This is the point at which the Western Christian must suspend his own worldview and traditions and examine the issue from the other's point of view. Is marriage finalized in the covenant made at engagement? Does the substantial down payment at engagement give a right to possess the woman? Or is it finalized when the last cow has been paid over? Is it finalized when the woman leaves her family's home to move to the home of her husband? Even if accepted as a normal happening, is sexual intercourse during the engagement period a distortion of the intended marriage process in this African culture? Or should the church marry couples before the bride price has been fully paid, to the consternation of traditional parents? What are the principles derived from the biblical narratives? There certainly is not one standard, prescribed marriage procedure recorded in the Scriptures.

These questions and contextual reflection require an adjustment to our normal manner of operating. The multicultural leader must learn when and how to step back and let another's point of view challenge and even alter his or her perspective.

To this point we have given attention to a Christian response to multiculturalism and have built a profile for leaders in multicultural congregations that reflects the ministry insights of multicultural practitioners. In this section we will integrate those observations with an evaluation tool for multicultural churches developed by Paul Pearce (2000). This reflection process allows the reader to develop a fuller understanding of both the goals of the multicultural congregation and the place of culturally sensitive leaders in shaping multi-ethnic congregations.

Observations from literature and research highlight the importance of personal life histories, multicultural self-awareness and intentionality in leaders of multi-ethnic congregations. *Personal life histories* reflect the significance of intercultural experiences, values developed in formative years, educational development, and attitudes toward difference. *Multicultural self-awareness* suggests the need for a personal understanding of intercultural knowledge as well as an ability to express a theology of diversity. *Intentionality* refers to a conscious desire to bring about transformation in intercultural relationships, particularly in the policies and practices of a community of faith. These three categories indicate the importance of ongoing development in the lives of leaders serving in multi-ethnic congregations.

On the basis of these findings, and in light of the profile already developed, we will build a matrix to enable congregational leaders to reflect upon their progress in multicultural self-awareness and to identify areas for further development. This matrix will form the basis for later discussion of processes useful in the ongoing development of multicultural self-awareness and competence in congregational leaders.

STAGES OF DEVELOPMENT FOR BECOMING A MULTICULTURAL CHURCH

In his doctoral dissertation (2000), Paul Pearce, a Canadian pastor, developed a continuum (see Fig. 2) for understanding the emergence of multicultural churches. His model was based upon work that was presented by Ronice E. Branding at a workshop organized by International Urban Associates (Chicago, 1993). This model also reflects the influence of Milton Bennett's *Developmental Stages of Intercultural Sensitivity*.[1]

The continuum describes congregations at six different stages of development toward the multicultural church. The continuum begins at one end with the term SEPARATION. The other end of the continuum refers to COMMUNITY (see Fig. 2). Pearce suggests that churches can be analyzed and placed somewhere on this scale according to their ministry vision and style. He identified the beginning point, *separation*, as referring to the manner in which the church interacts with difference. The monocultural church is "excluding," that is, it is a group which values the separation of the different ethnic and cultural groups. The end point of the continuum, *community*, typifies the multicultural, transformed church, which values a community inclusive of all ethnic or cultural groups.[2]

The chart at right (Fig. 2) summarizes Pearce's stages of institutional development toward the multicultural church. As he notes, churches moving along this continuum "will be experiencing attitudinal and structural changes that will be redefining their identity and mission."[3]

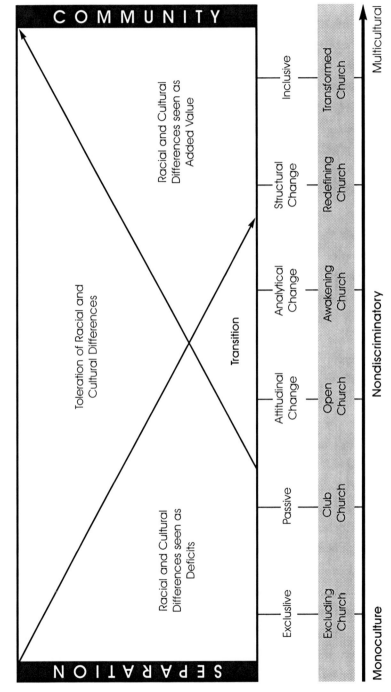

CONTINUUM ON BECOMING A MULTICULTURAL CHURCH

Figure 2 - [Paul Pearce, Ronice Branding, Milton Bennett]

At the separation end, **The Excluding Church** values exclusion as a means of preserving its identity and heritage. In this case, one ethnic or racial group intentionally embeds a monocultural environment through its teachings, decision-making, policies, informal practices and employment.

At the second stage, **The Club Church** maintains power and privilege for a dominant cultural group. It is tolerant of a limited number of "nice" people from other racial or ethnic groups. It does not believe there are any problems regarding diversity and may even view itself as multicultural because a few people from visible minorities attend the church.

At the third stage, **The Open Church** wants to be inclusive of all peoples but is often unaware of paternalistic attitudes and practices that maintain the privilege of the dominant group. People of other racial or ethnic groups are recruited for committees and may even be hired as support staff but changes in ministry style and practices are not seen as necessary. The Open Church is often visibly *multi-ethnic*.

At the fourth stage, **The Awakening Church** is more sensitive to discriminatory practices and is aware of the need for intentional intercultural dialogue within the congregation. It begins to examine infrastructures and policies that give advantages to the dominant group. Primary decision-making, however, still reflects the worldview of the dominant group. More and more people of different racial and ethnic backgrounds are feeling comfortable in the church.

At the fifth stage, **The Redefining Church** moves beyond tolerance and awareness to acceptance. It begins to see the benefits of a broader and more diverse racial and cultural perspective in its ministry. Intentional work is done to develop new policy and to re-structure the organization in a more inclusive manner. The congregation's primary decision-making strategies now have a multicultural character. Communication and conflict issues are dealt with in a manner that recognizes the diverse approaches present in the congregation.

At the sixth and final stage, **The Transformed Church** sees diversity as an asset; inclusion is central to the church's identity as a community of faith. At this stage, the church's life reflects diverse worldviews, contributions and interests in its mission, ministry style, policies and practices. Inclusive participation is understood in all the decisions that shape the church. Genuine intercultural community is seen and felt. The Transformed Church has become multicultural.[4]

This continuum of institutional stages of development toward the multicultural church provides a basis for understanding the developmental processes required for those who lead such congregations. To take this discussion a step further, we will now begin to look at the leaders of multi-ethnic congregations and examine the various stages of their development toward multicultural self-awareness.

CHAPTER 12

BECOMING A MULTICULTURAL LEADER

M any leaders in multi-ethnic churches express a desire to be more inclusive and intentional in their intercultural relationships. Likewise for the policies and practices of the congregations for which they have a level of responsibility. At the same time many express an undeveloped, or even convoluted, understanding of the issues at stake. For instance, one leader said:

> Let's let the other cultures stretch us, but let's get real, we are in the root culture and the immigrants who tend to evolve into leadership in our church acknowledge the importance of the dominant culture.

And again:

> If multiculturalism means let's have these side-by-side ghettos, so that you have a little Ghana here and little Pakistan here and little Croatia here, I don't want that.

Both statements reflect misunderstandings of a multicultural model and yet in practice this same leader affirmed a response which embraces diversity:

In some ways I have thoroughly bought into the mosaic idea, for example, the Ghanaians do things their way, special things with child christenings, etc. Fine, I wasn't going to fight that—saying, "you have to do it the way we do it." So there was that mosaic-ness and I wanted to bless that.

To see such leaders as participating in an ongoing process is more helpful than to locate them at a particular static point. It may be assumed that some Christian leaders in multi-ethnic churches have not yet opened themselves up to a readjustment process. Such leaders are most likely to be found in Exclusive, Passive or Open Churches.

In building a developmental matrix for multicultural leaders, Pearce's Multicultural Church stages have been used as a basis, with some modifications. Stages Four to Six (Redefining, Intentional and Inclusive) in the *Basic Form of Multicultural Developmental Matrix* (see Fig. 3, below) have been altered to reflect more personal development than organizational development (cf. Fig. 2, page 85).

Basic Form of Multicultural Developmental Matrix

Figure 3 - [Daniel R. Sheffield]

Profile Characteristics	Multicultural Stages Continuum					
	Exclusive	Passive	Open	Redefining	Intentional	Inclusive
Envisioning the Reality						
Embedding the Vision						
Embodying the Vision						
Embracing diversity						
Enabling empowerment	⟶					

TRANSFORMING WORLDVIEWS

It is helpful to understand where development and change takes place in the individual. The beginning point for increasing multicultural self-awareness is in the personal encounter. *Personal transformation* begins through positive encounters with persons of other cultures. For instance, David indicated:

> I grew up with guys from China and India, East Asians. I used to go to their homes and eat this great food. These guys were some of my best friends and we still keep in touch, even now... I always seem to gravitate to people of different backgrounds.

Personal transformation is limited, however, by the individual's ability to reflect on the significance of these encounters.

Cognitive transformation ensues as individuals redefine their attitudes and values on the basis of these personal encounters, as well as through interaction with literature and other resources that inform the redefinition process. Linda mentioned:

> If I see a person wearing a turban—well, I don't know many people that wear turbans... so if I knew someone well who wore a turban, I think my attitude and perhaps my fear, my hesitation to communicate, would be lessened...

And Pastor Jerry:

> I think that these various (cross-cultural) experiences have pre-disposed me to accepting different cultures and people on their own terms.

Cognitive transformation must then take root in inclusive practices.

Practical transformation happens as individuals commit themselves to meaningful intercultural relationships and submit themselves to multicultural group processes. Pastor Jack expressed his openness:

> It is through those people that we can be stretched and enriched, because we are starved relationally, we are starved affectively.

Becoming a Multicultural Leader: A Developmental Matrix

Figure 4 - [Daniel R. Sheffield]

Increasing Multicultural Self-Awareness →

Multicultural Stage Continuum

Personal transformation > Cognitive transformation > Practical transformation >

Profile	*Exclusive*	*Passive*	*Open*	*Redefining*	*Intentional*	*Inclusive*
Envisions Reality	sectarian; No reflection: "not an issue"	traditional; bounded reflection "no problem"	paternalistic; safe reflection: "is there a problem?"	aware of difference; new reflection; "Yes, there is a problem:"	accept difference; adjusted reflection; "What do we need to do?"	embrace difference; collective reflection; "this is our new way of doing things"
Embeds Vision	"God made us separate"	"they can come if they want"	"some of them are very nice people"	"God created us all uniquely	"God desires readjustment"	"we are transformed by adjustment"
Embodies The Vision	***************	appreciate power and privilege ***************	helping others feeds personal power; limited intercultural acquaintances	inviting others into power structures; developing intercultural friends	giving away power and privilege; regular intercultural social interaction	empowered by others; intercultural relationships normal
Embraces Diversity	***************	***************	begins to acquire cultural knowledge	cultural knowledge is "interesting"	cultural knowledge is "valued"; used in appropriate situations	cultural knowledge is "necessary" mutual critique
Enables Intercultural Dialogue	***************	***************	***************	recognize group processes are inadequate	finding intercultural dialogue resources	regular use of intercultural dialogue forms

Excluding — Tolerant → Nondiscriminatory — Accepting — Inclusive →

Monoculture — Multi-Ethnic → Nondiscriminatory → Multicultural

There are things we need desperately from them.

Susan commented on change in her church:

> We try and get the mix of people who are here also involved, because we do not want it to be just the one culture making all these decisions... we want a balance because there are so many cultures; we don't want it to be swayed by one side.

These personal aspects of development are then cross-referenced with the five *Multicultural Leader Profile* characteristics (developed in Section Two); that is, the attitudes, values and skills required of multicultural leaders.

STAGES IN LEADERSHIP TRANSFORMATION

This model for analysis draws together the five characteristics of the *Multicultural Leader Profile,* Pearce's continuum for *Becoming a Multicultural Church,* the literature on multicultural theory as well as social research observations. Figure 3 (p. 90) represents the two axes which are being cross-referenced. (Figure 4, left, represents the fully developed model.)

The following descriptions of leaders outline the various attitudes, values and skills found in the *Multicultural Leader Profile* at the different stages of multicultural development.

Stage One: The Exclusive Leader holds to a sectarian view of the Christian community. Since doctrine is a settled matter there is no need for ongoing reflection. Cultural diversity is not an issue because of the view that "God created us separate and that's the way it should stay." The excluding leader sees no reason to share power with someone who is not part of the exclusive community and has no dealings with persons of differing ethnic backgrounds. Intercultural sensitivity is non-existent and therefore intercultural empowerment skills are unnecessary.

Stage Two: The Passive Leader reflects a traditional view of the church in which the nature of the faith community is a fairly settled matter and reflection takes place within the boundaries of established norms. If racial integration is an accepted value in the denomination then this is affirmed. Passive leaders have no problem in regard to accepting others into their fellowship because they believe other ethnic people can come if they want to! They are comfortable with the level of power and privilege they wield in the life of the congregation and do not imagine that others might want to have a say in the affairs of the church. Intercultural relationships, cultural sensitivity and empowerment skills are not a part of their personal or ministry experience.

Stage Three: The Open Leader desires to be inclusive in the vision of the church but has limited intercultural experience and therefore tends to function paternalistically. Reflective thinking has broadened to include new information but still functions within the safe confines of expected ministry practice. The open leader is genuinely concerned about cross-cultural issues, but has a hard time believing there might be problems in the way people of other cultures experience the congregation. The open leader encourages congregational members to be warm towards persons of other cultures, and will say that "some of these are very nice people." Intercultural relations are at a limited acquaintanceship level. Deep friendships are unlikely. In fact, a kind of "helping out these people" approach actually tends to feed the self-worth of the dominant group person rather than vice versa. Persons of other cultures may be invited into committee structures primarily on the basis of outstanding gifts and abilities. In the course of limited contact the open leader may develop a base level of cultural knowledge and sensitivity, but has virtually no understanding of intercultural dialogue.

Stage Four: The Redefining Leader has become aware of cultural differences through personal encounters and begins to let these experiences affect ministry reflection processes. There is an acknowledgement that standard operating procedures in the congregation may cause problems for differing cultural viewpoints. There is recognition that God has created each person uniquely within the framework of a particular culture and this recognition initiates the development of a theology of diversity. The redefining leader actively draws people of other cultures into the decision-making structures of the congregation, recognizing the need to hear their voices. Intercultural friendships are developing and proving very rewarding. Cell and study groups are increasingly multi-ethnic. In interpersonal relations and committee meetings, cultural knowledge and sensitivity is increasing. Diverse viewpoints are "interesting" rather than "different." The different voice, however, may not yet have the weight to effect change in practices and attitudes in the wider congregation. Redefining leaders are coming to understand that "normal" dominant group processes are not adequate to encourage culturally different people to express their thoughts and spirituality. A search is begun to find more adequate intercultural knowledge and resources.

Stage Five: The Intentional Leader has moved beyond awareness to acceptance of cultural difference as a given in the nature of the Christian community. They have adjusted their critical reflection to be more "ethnorelative," i.e., recognizing difference without passing judgment. Intentional leaders are thinking proactively. They ask, "what do we need to do to correct our processes and reorient our structures to be more inclusive?" Primary decision-making is taking on a multicultural perspective as dominant group leaders give away power and privilege as a deliberate act of readjustment. The leadership community is actively developing intercultural friendships and freely interacts in informal social contexts. Almost all formal and informal groupings in the congregation function with cultural groups mixing freely. Communication issues and conflict situations actively utilize cultural knowledge and intercultural dialogue processes. Cultural knowledge is valued as a commodity. The intentional leader recognizes the need for greater understanding of intercultural dialogue and group dynamics. A variety of dialogue resources are being researched and developed in collaboration with other multicultural practitioners.

Stage Six: The Inclusive Leader sees difference as an asset to the faith community. These leaders have developed a vision of the multicultural congregation that essentially establishes a new norm for the nature of the church in the multi-ethnic urban environment. Diversity and inclusion become primary to the congregation's identity. The multicultural vision is articulated and demonstrated at all levels of congregational life, both public and communal. Power has been redistributed in a manner that allows all cultural groups to have a sense of ownership in congregational life. The inclusive leader has moved from a position of power to recognizing servanthood as the means of empowering those who have formerly been disadvantaged and disempowered. Authentic intercultural relationships have become a way of life and embody the vision in the heart and soul of the congregation. The inclusive leader has learned the deeply spiritual activity of "mutual critique." Giving and receiving constructive criticism calls for adjustment of identity around culturally determined values and practices, and the negotiation of shared meanings. These leaders are increasingly utilizing processes that enable and empower the inclusive, multicultural vision to take root in practical ways in the congregation. They are developing their own unique forms of interaction through regular collaboration with other multicultural practitioners. These forms allow meaningful understanding and depth of community to come to life.

USEFULNESS OF A DEVELOPMENTAL MATRIX FOR MULTICULTURAL LEADERS

This matrix (Fig. 4) is helpful in visualizing the issues that need to be addressed by leaders to determine their present position and a direction for future development. Leaders functioning in multi-ethnic congregations need to assess where they fit in this matrix and determine whether there is a desire and will to begin the process of intercultural development.

As leaders take steps toward more inclusive practices there are a variety of resources beneficial for self-reflection as well as collaborative learning opportunities, and the matrix enables assessment of such resources in light of one's present developmental position. For leaders

96

in multicultural ministry who are seeking to empower other leaders, the matrix gives direction for appropriate training targets.

Beyond individual leaders, the matrix is also a useful tool for church search committees. The multicultural congregation can use the matrix in assessing both potential pastoral candidates as well as for nominating lay ministry leaders. Denominational leaders who have responsibility for assessing and recommending potential pastors for multi-ethnic congregations will also find the developmental matrix of value. The matrix can indicate the pastor appropriate for a congregation by comparison with the congregation's current position on Pearce's multicultural church continuum.

The matrix for multicultural leaders finally leads us to examine the appropriate means for stimulating the development of such leaders. In the following chapter we will suggest a model that addresses the need for personal self-reflection and intercultural experience as well as for collaborative learning opportunities.

CHAPTER 13

DEVELOPING A CATHOLIC PERSONALITY

So far we have found several focus areas in the developmental process leading from exclusive to inclusive leadership. It appears that the most significant catalysts for growth in multicultural self-awareness are:

• *Meaningful intercultural relationships:* that causes reflection on attitudes regarding difference

• *Cultural knowledge, experience and resources:* that develops understanding and sensitivity

• *Reflective input for alternative theology and practice:* that challenges status quo thought and practice

• *Collaborative learning processes:* that affirms, empowers and resources ministry through dialogue with other multicultural leaders

Leaders for multicultural congregations must go through a personal process of adjustment. This adjustment will require destabilizing periods of cultural ineptitude, anger and frustration. It will require a conscious searching out of new ways to see previously held paradigms and accepted knowledge. It will require the acquisition of new cultural knowledge and new patterns of seeing, hearing, and expressing. It is this process of adjustment and transformation that produces "the catholic personality."

In order to encourage the ongoing development of leaders in multicultural congregations I want to look at these transformative factors through the lens of adult learning models.

Leaders in multicultural congregations are ministry practitioners; that is, they are people actively involved in the face-to-face practice of intercultural dialogue and the development of policies and processes that enable such dialogue in a multi-ethnic organization. Multicultural leaders must educate themselves and other leaders in their congregations if growth towards inclusion is to be realized in their congregations. In this chapter we will review concepts that deal specifically with adult learning and particularly with critical reflection processes for practitioners. These processes can help leaders intentionally move through the different stages outlined in the *Multicultural Developmental Matrix*.

THE REFLECTIVE PRACTITIONER

The *reflective practitioner* is a concept provided by Donald Schon (1983, 1987) that highlights an individual, self-directed, experience-based professional learning and developmental process for the practitioner. Schon's model is a departure from the 'technocratic model' for developing professional expertise which assumed that problem-solving can be mastered primarily through rigorous application of a proven discipline of knowledge, theories and techniques. In the present fast changing society, however, knowledge is evolving at a rate beyond normal assimilation and the context of practice is continually being modified. Schon's model, therefore, enables the leader to keep pace with change by suggesting a means that encourages critical reflection during or after a particular activity.

Schon calls for practitioners who will critically analyze, make informed judgments and redirect their actions while they are engaged in the activity they wish to reflect upon. This ability for reflection is "the result of the combination of experience, propositional knowledge, tacit knowledge or know how, critical thinking and other kinds of process and intuitive knowledge which have been developed through previous reflections."[1]

The process of reflection, according to Schon, includes four movements: knowing-in-action, comprehending a dilemma, reflection-in-action, and modified action. Reflection-on-action takes place after an activity. Generally practitioners are guided by tacit knowledge (know-how/craft) that is adapted and used in the course of an activity (see Fig. 5). Schon refers to this tacit knowledge as *knowing-in-action*. It is an implicit process of adaptation.[2] Practitioners use present knowledge in a manner that has worked in the past, merely adjusting for a new circumstance. This knowing-in-action, however, can become unthinking and routine, therefore implicit processes need to be made explicit so that reflection can occur. Suppose a typical activity does not provide the necessary solutions to a given situation. The practitioner may be surprised by a failure or mismatch in his or her reaction to the situation. Tacit knowledge or the knowing-in-action process has not provided sufficient information to respond to the situation. Schon describes this as a *dilemma* or moment of surprise. In the immediate context of an activity—what Schon's refers to as "action-present"—critical reflection on tacit knowledge may occur, thus creating new understandings that are made explicit, reprocessed

Schon's Reflective Practitioner
Figure 5 - [Daniel R. Sheffield]

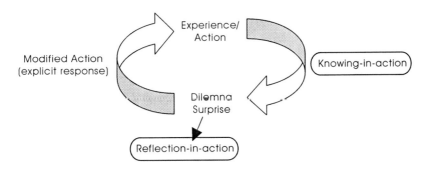

Experience/Action

Knowing-in-action

Modified Action (explicit response)

Dilemna Surprise

Reflection-in-action

and reinforced or modified. It is these moments of *reflection-in-action* that Schon claims are the core of the 'art' of expertise.[3] *Reflection-on-action* takes place when the practitioner conducts a kind of 'post-mortem' sometime after the experience has passed.

Schon's model is quite helpful, but a number of critics have wondered whether this model actually helps leaders to change their practices. Is personal critical reflection enough to produce significant change? In the *Cambridge Journal of Education*, college lecturer Andy Convery (1998) provides an insightful critique of Schon's methodology. Convery suggests that while Schon's principle of reflection-in-action has application to the teaching profession, the self-reflective process often has limited ability in resolving teachers' difficulties.[4] He feels that by using Schon's model individual teachers may feel they have in fact been reflecting critically and thus misleading themselves and not improving their practice at all.[5]

Convery feels that Schon's reflection-in-action implies "that some personal tinkering or some individual problem solving can activate the professional in the teacher," offering the illusion of independent, self-improvement.[6] Convery's point is that individuals "are unlikely to make essential changes to their practice if they are not supported and guided through the reflective process."[7] Unless reflection is informed by collaborative discussion, individual reflection tends to focus on immediate rather than underlying problems.[8]

The Reflective Practitioner model is valuable for understanding the development of attitudes, values and skills in congregational leaders in multi-ethnic settings. It highlights the need for ongoing reflection that is not based solely upon a certain set of values and skills acquired in a training environment. Interaction with people of differing cultural backgrounds requires constant adjustment in the leader. Adjusting habits and practices within a known framework (knowing-in-action) is not sufficient by itself—critical reflection on existing practices must also take place. With time and experience this reflection-in-action can become a valuable skill for the multicultural leader, increasing their intercultural and interpersonal expertise.

However, as Convery notes, individual self-reflection (in this case, on intercultural practice) is often not enough. There is a need to move beyond a limited reflective context of problem-solving to engage with others who can challenge practitioner-leaders to look outside of their present individual capacity and frame of reference for behaviour and practice. That is, learning and reflecting must actually transform the leader so that he or she moves through the developmental matrix. To the extent that the self-reflection model achieves this, it is useful for development in understanding and practices.

TRANSFORMATIVE LEARNING

Another model that highlights the importance of critical reflection on practice is Jack Mezirow's model for *transformative learning* (1991). From his perspective, the goal of adult learning is to enable people to make their own interpretations of their experiences rather than acting upon the purposes, beliefs, judgments and feelings of others. Transformative learning focuses on the centrality of experience, critical reflection and rational discourse. Learners begin to change their "meaning schemes" (specific beliefs, attitudes, and emotional reactions) as they engage in critical reflection upon their experiences. This leads, in turn, to a transformation of perspective, a realignment of one's "meaning structure," or worldview.[9] Transformation, says Mezirow, includes "the process of becoming critically aware of how and why our assumptions have come to constrain the way we perceive, understand, and feel about our world; changing these structures of habitual expectation to make possible a more inclusive, discriminating, and integrating perspective; and finally, making choices or otherwise acting upon these new understandings."[10]

The beliefs, attitudes and emotional reactions that make up an individual's micro meaning schemes are constantly being adjusted and transformed through normal learning processes. People change through their life experiences. These small adjustments to beliefs, attitudes and reactions, however, are set within a meaning structure, or frame of reference, that inevitably limits the degree of transformation possible. Mezirow suggests that these micro-adjustments seldom affect our worldview, or in his terms, our meaning structure. A transformation of perspective, that upsets the existing, macro, meaning structure, happens infrequently. But it is this experience of disturbance to the wider meaning structures that leads to transformation. Mezirow believes that transformation is usually the result of a "disorienting dilemma" that is triggered by a life crisis or a major life transition, although it may result from an accumulation of micro transformations in meaning schemes over a period of time.[11] Transformative learning, therefore, occurs when individuals change their frames of reference (meaning structures) by critically reflecting on their assumptions and beliefs and by implementing plans that bring about new ways of defining their worlds.

In a modification to Mezirow's model put forward by Robert Boyd, the process of discernment is central to transformation (Figure 6). Discernment requires extra-rational sources such as symbols, images, and archetypes to assist in creating personal meaning.[12] In Boyd's model, grieving is the most critical phase of the discernment process. Grieving involves both cognitive and emotional elements of change. Grieving occurs when an individual begins to realize that old patterns and ways of perceiving are no longer relevant and moves to adopt or establish new ways, integrating old and new patterns.[13]

The integrated model of Transformative Learning (Fig. 6) provides some helpful insights for leaders in multi-ethnic congregations. The leader in the multicultural congregation must pass through these stages of disorientation, self-examination, grieving, adjustment and reorganization if he or she is to be effective in overseeing an inclusive community of faith.

In many mono-cultural congregations, the entrance of persons of diverse ethnic backgrounds is a disorienting experience and sooner or later it also becomes a dilemma, a challenge to the existing way of doing things. By including the concept of grieving in the transformation process, we are able to understand more fully the depth of challenge that the encounter of difference is to many individuals at the affective

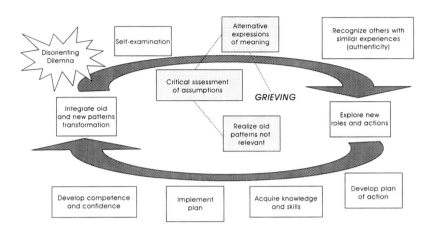

Transformative Learning (Mezirow and Boyd)
Figure 6 - [Daniel R. Sheffield]

level. As long-time congregational members come to understand that cultural diversity has become a reality in their community, they must grieve the loss of their traditional way of relating. This is also true for the leader of such a process. Often personal disappointment, anger or failure in relating to people of other cultures will trigger a profound disorientation.

Mezirow raises the need for connection with others who have gone, or a going through, similar experiences. Kathleen Loughlin, a transformative learning practitioner, talks about the importance of creating "a community of knowers," individuals who are "united in a shared experience of trying to make meaning of their life experience."[14] This corresponds with Convery's critique of reflection-in-action; that is, that a collaborative model is of importance to the learning process. In the case of the multi-ethnic congregation, the transformation to functioning multiculturally needs to be done at the collective level as well as at the individual level.

COLLABORATIVE LEARNING

In Convery's critique of Schon, he argues that "for constructive self-reflection, (learners) need to believe they have the support of others who will sufficiently respect the integrity of their enquiry to enable awkward and uncomfortable self-revelations to be identified."[15] These awkward experiences will often include grieving the loss of a previous way of thinking. In language similar to Mezirow's transformative learning process, Convery identified in his own experience that "a sympathetic audience enabled me to re-frame the problem."[16] Convery describes a process that involves the necessity of confrontation, either by self or others, that goes beyond cognitive activity, in which individuals may experience feelings of instability, anxiety, negativity and even depression.[17] This is reminiscent of Mezirow's "disorienting dilemma" and Boyd's "grieving" experience. This kind of self-evaluation is highly emotional and learners may be tempted to retreat and thus endanger further learning.

Stephen Brookfield in *Becoming a Critically Reflective Teacher* (1995), relates the importance of collaborative learning for developing the professional practice of teachers. Critical reflection, he says, requires that conditions be created under which each person is respected, valued and heard. For adult professional development this means an engagement in critical conversation.[18]

To become critically reflective, Brookfield suggests that we must see our practice through several lenses; through our own autobiographies, through the eyes of the learners we work with, through the experiences of our professional colleagues, and through the encounter with theoretical literature.[19] In examining our own autobiographies we often find that we are more influenced by our *experiences* as learners than by sound pedagogic method. Through personal self-reflection we become aware of paradigm assumptions and instinctive reasoning that frame the way that we think and work. When we have a clearer understanding of these personal processes then we can test them against the perspective of other learners, colleagues and against theory (see Figure 7).[20]

The practice of collaborative learning highlights the importance of creating an environment of support and care where individuals are respected, heard and valued, and from which constructive

Critical Reflection Components

Figure 7 - [Daniel R. Sheffield]

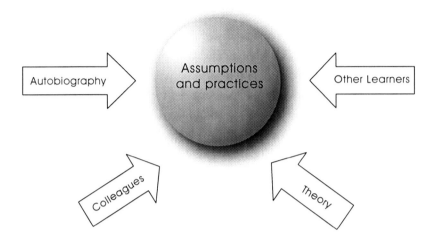

dialogue and adjusted practice can proceed. Leaders in multi-ethnic congregations are often struggling with their own personal adjustment to worldviews that challenge the way they have always seen things. They are struggling with congregational policies and practices that often exclude differing ways of experiencing the meaning of being the body of Christ. The collaborative learning model can be useful in pointing the way forward in such a collective body as the church, through constructive dialogue. Individual reflection and adjustment is necessary, but ultimately the wider group and its policies and practices must also undergo analysis, constructive criticism and adjustment.

LEARNING PROCESSES
FOR MULTICULTURAL LEADERS

In the introduction to this chapter we indicated the need of multicultural leaders for learning processes which address needs for a) personal self-reflection; b) transformative intercultural experiences; and c) collaborative learning opportunities. The educational methods that have been examined form a foundation for such processes. On one hand, to say that one of these methods addresses every conceivable need or best articulates the development process is inappropriate, as their critics have identified. On the other hand, these models do highlight particular issues of concern in a developmental understanding of growth, change and transformation.

Leaders in multi-ethnic congregations would profit from learning experiences that provide for *personal self-reflection*. Reflection on personal assumptions, habits and practices regarding ethnic diversity will only enable leaders to adjust such assumptions, habits and practices within a limited frame. This adjustment is limited to the extent that the individual can conceptualize a different way of seeing, through past training and current knowledge. There needs to be challenge and input from outside the leader's present experience. In the context of the multi-ethnic congregation this challenge will come as leaders open themselves to dealing authentically with differing worldviews.

The *authentic transformative encounter* with a person of another culture involves respecting that person's cultural frame as a valid way of seeing the world. It means valuing the worth of that person as a unique creation in God's eyes, even before adoption into the body of Christ, as well as genuinely hearing the concerns of that person as a legitimate voice in the community of faith. This kind of encounter is often disorienting, affecting the leader at both the cognitive and affective levels.

For transformation to happen in leaders and, by eventual extrapolation, in the congregations which they lead, adjustment will come via working through the implications of the disorienting encounter. This adjustment can often be done most helpfully in a *collaborative learning environment* with other leaders working on the same concerns. The adjustment process involves grieving the loss of one way of seeing the world, exploring new ways of thinking and acting, and then acquiring new knowledge and skills. Multicultural leaders must develop confidence and competence in thinking and acting in the context of making these adjustments. Finally this learning process requires integrating old and new ways of seeing that admit to new dimensions of understanding without negating the value and meaning of previously held understandings.

Throughout this book I have sought to identify practical issues which can aid leaders in multicultural congregations. The foundations of an acquired theology of diversity are invaluable. We must build a model that reflects the character of God and his expressed desire to see all *ethne* represented in his kingdom. We must be able to articulate a theology which requires inclusive heterogeneity, rather than exclusive homogeneity. The body of Christ is to be recognized most clearly where all people groups are functioning in harmony and relationship with one another, learning from one another and adjusting, rather than staying in compartmentalized groups of likeminded people.

In defining the qualities of the multicultural leader, I have sought to reflect the best practices of such leaders, acquired through experience, observation, interviews and literature surveys. This leadership role is one of intentionality. The five E's (envision, embed, embody, embrace, enable) do not come naturally—our natural inclination is to conduct business as usual. But the comfortability of the status quo is not acceptable in our spiritual lives and therefore should not be acceptable in the practices of the Christian congregation.

Becoming a multicultural leader and developing the catholic, embracing, personality is an ongoing task. We need to make use of tools and approaches to transformation that enable our development and adjustment. The stages of development toward inclusiveness that have been outlined assure us that forward movement is possible. Adjustment is possible if we are prepared for the work of critical reflection on our assumptions and behaviours; to become more fully engaged with the transforming and inclusive God of Christian Scripture.

NOTES

CHAPTER 1

[1] Judith Gundry-Volf and Miroslav Volf, *A Spacious Heart: Essays on Identity and Belonging* (Harrisburg, PA: Trinity Press International, 1997), 9.

[2] Gerald Arbuckle, *Earthing the Gospel: An Inculturation Handbook for the Pastoral Worker* (Maryknoll, NY: Orbis Books, 1990), 180.

[3] Arbuckle, *Earthing the Gospel*, 180.

[4] Ibid., 181.

[5] Gerald Arbuckle, a Marist priest from New Zealand, is a leading theologian and anthropologist with extensive experience in Southeast Asia and Australia. His book *Earthing the Gospel* (1990) is particularly valuable for ministry practitioners.

[6] Charles Taylor is Professor of Philosophy and Political Science at McGill University in Montreal.

[7] Charles Taylor, "The Politics of Recognition" in *Multiculturalism: Examining The Politics of Recognition,* edited by Amy Gutman. (Princeton: Princeton University Press, 1994), 38.

[8] Taylor, "Politics of Recognition," 39.

[9] Ibid., 43.

[10] Steven Rockefeller, "Comment" in *Multiculturalism: Examining the Politics of Recognition,* edited by Amy Gutman. (Princeton: Princeton University Press, 1994), 92.

[11] Taylor, "Politics of Recognition," 62.

[12] James Lynch, *Multicultural Education: Principles and Practice* (London: Routledge and Keagan, 1986), 15.

[13] Arturo Escobar, *Encountering Development* (Princeton, NJ: Princeton University Press, 1995), 218.

[14] Escobar, 1995, 219.

[15] Lynch, 1986, 6.

[16] Tim Schouls, *Shifting Boundaries: Aboriginal Identity, Pluralist Theory and the Politics of Self-Government* (Vancouver: University of British Columbia Press, 2003), 172.

[17] Donald McGavran, *Understanding Church Growth* (Grand Rapids: Eerdmans, 1970).

[18] Charles Foster, *Embracing Diversity: Leadership in Multicultural Congregations.* (Washington, DC: The Alban Institute, 1997), 24.

[19] Foster, 1997, 26.

[20] Foster, 1997, 25.

CHAPTER 2

[1] Richard Mouw in Boulton, Wayne, Kennedy, Thomas and Verhey, Allen, eds. *From Christ to the World: Introductory Readings in Christian Ethics* (Grand Rapids: Eerdmans, 1994), 32.

[2] Mouw in Boulton, 1994, 32.

[3] Henri Blocher, *In the Beginning: The Opening Chapters of Genesis* (Downers Grove, IL: Inter-Varsity Press, 1984), 203.

[4] Stanley Hauerwas in Stephen Rhodes, *Where the Nations Meet: the Church in a multicultural world* (Downers Grove, IL: Intervarsity Press, 1998), 27.

[5] John R.W. Stott, *God's New Society: The Message of Ephesians* (Downers Grove, Ill.: InterVarsity Press, 1979), 92.

[6] Ibid., 103.

[7] Miroslav Volf, *Exclusion and Embrace: a theological exploration of identity, otherness and reconciliation* (Nashville: Abingdon Press, 1996), 48.

CHAPTER 3

[1] Boulton, *From Christ to the World*, 5.

[2] Boulton, *From Christ to the World*, 231.

[3] Nicholas Wolterstorff in Boulton et al. 1994, 251.

[4] Wolterstorff in Boulton, et al. 1994, 252.

[5] Rhodes, 1998, 46.

[6] Volf, 1996, 40.

[7] Ibid., 48.

[8] Ibid., 49.

[9] Volf, 1996, 51.

[10] Miroslav Volf in Gundry-Volf, 1997, 44.

[11] Stanley Hauerwas. *A Community of Character: Toward a Constructive Christian Social Ethic* (Notre Dame, IN: University of Notre Dame Press, 1981), 3.

[12] John Howard Yoder, *The Politics of Jesus* (Grand Rapids: Eerdmans Publishing, 1972), 97.

[13] Parker Palmer, *The Company of Strangers: Christians and the Renewal of America's Public Life* (Crossroad Publishing, 1983), 64.

[14] Ibid., 28.

[15] Rhodes 1998, 76.

[16] John Perkins, *Beyond Charity: The Call to Christian Community Development* (Grand Rapids: Baker Book House, 1993), 49.

CHAPTER 4

[1] 86.9% of visible minorities in Canada live in British Columbia, Ontario and Quebec. The vast majority of these (80-90%) live in the urban centres of Vancouver, Toronto and Montreal. ("Immigration and Discrimination: a challenge for the Church," *Context,* Fall 1998, Vol.7, No. 4).

[2] John Leonard, "The Church in between cultures." *Evangelical Missions Quarterly*, January 2004, 62-70.

[3] For instance: R. Bibby, *Mosaic Madness* (Toronto: Stoddard Publishing, 1990); S.D. Gaede, *When Tolerance is No Virtue* (Downer's Grove, IL: Intervarsity Press, 1995); J.D. Hunter, *Culture Wars: The Struggle to Define America* (New York: Basic Books, 1991).

[4] Donald Posterski. *True to You* (Winfield, BC: Wood Lake Books, 1995), 89.

[5] Posterski, *True to You*, 156-157.

[6] Rhodes, 1998, 46.

[7] Stanley Hauerwas and William Willimon, *Resident Aliens: Life in the Christian Colony* (Nashville: Abingdon Press, 1989), 42-43.

[8] Volf, 1996, 110.

CHAPTER 5

[1] I suggest that all Christian congregations should embrace the basic convictions of multiculturalism. In the development of actual ministry philosophy, strategy and practices, some churches in multi-ethnic contexts may feel that homogeneous, ethnic, first-language congregations are the most effective for their focus audience. While this is a valid strategy, ministry leaders must be aware of the sociological realities of second-generation integration with the host culture which often leads to a movement away from ethnic churches. Such ethnic churches must maintain a broader understanding of multicultural issues and build relationships with multicultural congregations in which their integrating second-generation can develop an adjusted faith identity that is not bound to a particular culture.

[2] Howard Gardner in Charles Foster, *Embracing Diversity: Leadership in*

Multicultural Congregations (Washington, DC: The Alban Institute, 1997), 116.
[3] Foster 1997, 1

CHAPTER 6

[1] Howard Gardner, professor of education at Harvard, developer of the "multiple intelligences" model of education, gave his attention to leadership studies in *Leading Minds: An Anatomy of Leadership* (1995).
[2] Howard Gardner, "A Cognitive View of Leadership," *Education Week.* Vol.15:2, 1995b, 34.
[3] Gardner 1995b, 35.
[4] Howard Gardner, *Leading Minds: An Anatomy of Leadership* (New York: Basic Books, 1995), 9-11
[5] Gardner 1995b, 35
[6] Hauerwas and Willimon, are both professors at Duke University Divinity School in North Carolina. They function within the mainstream Methodist tradition.
[7] Stanley Hauerwas and William Willimon, *Resident Aliens: Life in the Christian Colony* (Nashville: Abingdon Press,1989), 112
[8] Hauerwas 1989, 47.
[9] Hauerwas 1989, 47.
[10] Hauerwas 1989, 138-139.

CHAPTER 7

[1] Edgar Schein was professor of management studies at Massachusetts Institute of Technology (MIT) at the time he wrote *Organizational Culture and Leadership* in 1985. Schein has written on organizational psychology and dynamics as well as management theory and leadership practices dating back to the 1960s.
[2] In the fields of psychology and sociology, the study of organizational culture often uses culture-change or culture-transmission as a verb, rather than using the adverb "cultural" to define the verb "change."
[3] Edgar Schein, *Organizational Culture and Leadership* (San Francisco: Jossey-Bass Publishers 1985), 223
[4] Schein 1985, 224-225.
[5] Schein 1985, 316.
[6] Schein 1985, 317.
[7] Schein 1985, 317.
[8] Schein 1985, 324.
[9] Schein 1985, 325.

[10] Schein 1985, 326.

CHAPTER 8

[1] Gardner 1995b, 35.

[2] Gardner 1995b, 34.

[3] Eric Law, an Episcopal priest, is a professional consultant in the area of multicultural leadership and organizational development, presently based in Vancouver, BC.

[4] Eric Law, *The Wolf Shall Dwell With the Lamb: a spirituality for leadership in a multicultural community* (St. Louis: Chalice Press, 1993), 42-43.

CHAPTER 9

[1] Charles Foster is professor of religion and education at the Candler School of Theology of Emory University, Atlanta Georgia.

[2] Foster 1997, 118.

[3] Foster 1997, 118.

[4] Foster 1997, 118.

[5] Foster 1997, 118.

[6] Foster 1997, Sharon Welch, "An Ethic of Solidarity and Difference" in Henry A. Giroux, ed. *Postmodernism, Feminism and Cultural Politics: Redrawing Education Boundaries* (Albany: State University of New York Press, 1991).

[7] Foster 1997, 47.

[8] Foster 1997, 69.

[9] Foster 1997, 70.

[10] Raleigh Washington and Glen Kehrein, *Breaking Down Walls* (Chicago: Moody Press, 1993), 131-133.

[11] Foster 1997, 119-120.

[12] Welch 1991, 89.

[13] Foster 1997, 121.

[14] David Augsberger, author of *Pastoral Counseling Across Cultures* (Philadelphia: Westminster Press, 1986), refers to this process as "interpathy" in Foster, 1997, 122.

[15] Foster 1997, 122.

CHAPTER 10

[1] In his book, *Natural Church Development* (1996), German church consultant Christian Schwarz builds upon quantitative research conducted in more than 1000 churches in 32 different countries around the world. His research enabled the development of an index of 8 qualities essential to healthy church life.

[2] Christian Schwarz, *Natural Church Development* (Winfield, BC: International Centre for Leadership Development and Evangelism, 1996), 22

[3] Schwarz 1996, 23.

[4] Schwarz 1996, 22.

[5] Schwarz 1996, 22.

[6] Gardner 1995b, 35.

[7] Schwarz 1996, 23.

[8] Law 1993, 30.

[9] Law 1993, 31-32.

[10] Law 1993, 35.

[11] Law 1993, 36.

[12] Hauerwas 1989, 139.

[13] Hauerwas 1989, 113.

[14] Miroslav Volf, *Exclusion and Embrace: A theological exploration of identity, otherness and reconciliation* (Nashville: Abingdon Press, 1995), 51.

CHAPTER 11

[1] M.J. Bennett, "Towards ethnorelativism: A developmental model of intercultural sensitivity," in *Education for the Intercultural Experience*, 2nd ed. (Yarmouth, ME: Intercultural Press, 1993). Bennett uses the following six terms to describe the developmental stages: Denial, Defense, Minimization, Acceptance, Adaptation, Integration.

[2] Paul Pearce, "Characteristics of Emerging Healthy Multicultural Churches." D.Min. dissertation, McMaster Divinity College, McMaster University, 2000, 141.

[3] Pearce, 2000, 144.

[4] Pearce, 2000, 144-147.

CHAPTER 13

[1] Regina Hatten, Knapp, R.D. and Salonga, R. "Action Research: Comparison with the concepts of 'The Reflective Practitioner' and 'Quality Assurance' in I. Hughes, ed. *Action Research Electronic Reader,* The Universityof Sydney, online <http://www.cchs.usyd.edu.au/arow/reader/rdr.htm>, 1997, 6.

[2] Donald Schon, *The Reflective Practitioner* (New York: Basic Books,1983), 49.

[3] Donald Schon, ed. *The Reflective Turn: Case Studies in and on Educational Practice* (New York: Teacher College Press, 1991), 50.

[4] Andy Convery, "A Teacher's Response to 'Reflection-in-Action,'" *Cambridge Journal of Education* (Vol. 28:2 June 1998:197-106), 197.

[5] Convery 1998, 198-199.

[6] Convery 1998, 201.

[7] Convery 1998, 201.

[8] Convery 1998, 197.

[9] Jack Mezirow, *Transformative Dimensions in Adult Learning* (San Francisco: Jossey-Bass, 1991), 167.

[10] Mezirow 1991, 167.

[11] Jack Mezirow, "Transformation Theory of Adult Learning" in *In Defence of the Lifeworld,* edited by M.R. Welton, 39-70, (New York: SUNY Press, 1995), 50.

[12] Susan Imel "Transformative Learning in Adulthood," *ERIC Digest* No. 200 (Columbus, OH: ERIC Clearinghouse on Adult, Career and Vocational Education, College of Education, Ohio State University, 1998), 2.

[13] Imel 1998, 3.

[14] Kathleen Loughlin, *Women's Perceptions of Transformative Learning Experiences within Consciousness-Raising* (San Francisco: Mellen Research University Press, 1993), 320-321.

[15] Convery 1998, 201.

[16] Convery 1998, 201.

[17] Convery 1998, 202.

[18] Stephen Brookfield, *Becoming a Critically Reflective Teacher* (San Francisco: Jossey-Bass, 1995), 27.

[19] Brookfield 1995, 29.

[20] Brookfield 1995, 29.

SELECT BIBLIOGRAPHY

Arbuckle, Gerald, *Earthing the Gospel: An Inculturation Handbook for the Pastoral Worker.* Maryknoll, NY: Orbis Books, 1990.

Bennett, Milton. "Towards ethnorelativism: A developmental model of intercultural sensitivity" in *Education for the Intercultural Experience* (2nd ed.) Yarmouth, ME: Intercultural Press, 1993.

Bibby, Reginald. *Mosaic Madness.* Toronto: Stoddart Publishing Co. Ltd., 1990.

Claerbaut, David. *Urban Ministry.* Grand Rapids: Zondervan, 1984.

Cloke, P., Philo, C. and Sadler, D. (eds) *Approaching Human Geography: an introduction to contemporary theoretical debates.* London: Paul Chapman Publishing, 1991.

Earle, R.L. and Wirth, J.D (eds.) *Identities in North America: The Search for Community.* Stanford,Ca: Stanford University Press, 1995.

Elmer, Duane. *Cross-Cultural Conflict.* Downers Grove: Intervarsity Press, 1995.

Fine, Marlene. *Building Successful Multicultural Organizations: challenges and opportunities.* London: Quorum Books, 1995.

Foster, Charles. *Embracing Diversity: Leadership in Multicultural Congregations.* Washington, D.C.: The Alban Institute, 1997.

_____ and Brelsford, Theodore. *We Are The Church Together: Cultural Diversity in Congregational Life.* Valley Forge, PA: Trinity Press, 1996.

Goldberg, David. (editor) *Multiculturalism: a critical reader.* Boston: Blackwell Publishing, 1994.

Gundry-Volf, Judith and Volf, Miroslav. *A Spacious Heart: Essays on Identity and Belonging.* Harrisburg, PA: Trinity Press International, 1997.

Hauerwas, Stanley. *A Community of Character: Toward a Constructive Christian Social Ethic.* Notre Dame, IN: University of Notre Dame Press, 1981.

Hauwerwas, S. and Willimon, W. *Resident Aliens: Life in the Christian Colony.* Nashville: Abingdon Press, 1989.

Hays, J. Daniel. *From Every People and Nation: A Biblical Theology of Race.* Downers Grove: Apollo/Intervarsity Press, 2003.

Hughes, Dewi. "Ethnicity and Globalization" a paper presented at the Global Connections Conference. Swanwick, England, 2002.

Koyama, Kosuke. *Water Buffalo Theology.* Maryknoll: Orbis Books, 1999.

Law, Eric H.F. *The Bush Was Blazing But Not Consumed: developing a multicultural community through dialogue and liturgy.* St. Louis: Chalice Press, 1996.

_____. *The Wolf Shall Dwell With the Lamb: a spirituality for leadership in a multicultural community.* St. Louis: Chalice Press, 1993.

Lee, Jung Young. *Marginality: the key to multi-cultural theology.* Minneapolis: Fortress Press, 1995.

Leonard, John. "The Church in between cultures." Evangelical Missions Quarterly, January 2004, pp. 62-70.

Lingenfelter, Sherwood. *Transforming Culture: a challenge for Christian mission.* Grand Rapids: Baker Book House, 1992.

Lupton, Robert. *Theirs Is The Kingdom: Celebrating the Gospel in Urban America.* San Francisco: Harper, 1989.

McGavran, Donald. *Understanding Church Growth.* Grand Rapids: Eerdmans, 1970.

Newbigin, Lesslie. *The Open Secret: An Introduction to the Theology of Mission (rev. ed).* Grand Rapids: Baker Books, 1995.

Niebuhr, Richard. *Christ and Culture.* New York: Harper Publishing, 1951.

Ortiz, Manuel. One New People: *Models for Developing a Multi-ethnic Church.* Downers Grove: InterVarsity Press, 1996.

Palmer, Parker. *The Company of Strangers: Christians and the Renewal of America's Public Life.* Crossroad Publishing, 1983.

Perkins, John. *With Justice for All.* Ventura, Calif.: Regal, 1982.

_____. *Beyond Charity: The Call to Christian Community Development.* Grand Rapids: Baker Book House, 1993.

Posterski, Donald. *True to You.* Winfield, BC: Wood Lake Books, 1995.

_____. *Enemies with Smiling Faces: Defeating the Subtle Threats that Endanger Christians.* Downers Grove: Intervarsity Press, 2004.

Rhodes, Stephen A. *Where the Nations Meet: the Church in a multicultural world.* Downers Grove, Ill: Intervarsity Press, 1998.

Sanneh, Lamin. *Encountering the West: Christianity and the Global Cultural Process*. New York: Orbis Books, 1993.

Schaller, Lyle. *The Change Agent: The Strategy of Innovative Leadership*. Nashville: Abingdon Press, 1972.

Schein, Edgar H. *Organizational Culture and Leadership*. San Francisco: Jossey-Bass Publishers, 1985.

Schouls, Tim. *Shifting Boundaries: Aboriginal Identity, Pluralist Theory and the Politics of Self-Government*. Vancouver: University of British Columbia Press, 2003.

Sheffield, Dan and Joyce Bellous. "Learning to Be a Missionary" in World Evangelical Alliance Resources. <www.wearesources.org/publications.aspx> (2003).

Sheffield, Dan and Kathleen. "Ubunye Church and Community Ministries" in *Serving with the Urban Poor*, edited by: T. Yamamori, B. Myers, K. Luscombe. Monrovia: MARC (World Vision), 1998.

Shorter, Aylward. *The Church in the African City*. London: Geoffrey Chapman, 1991.

Taylor, Charles. "The Politics of Recognition" in *Multiculturalism: Examining The Politics of Recognition*, edited by Amy Gutman. Princeton: Princeton University Press, 1994.

Volf, Miroslav. *Exclusion and Embrace: A theological exploration of identity, otherness and reconciliation*. Nashville: Abingdon Press, 1996.

Venter, Dawid. "The Inverted Norm: the formation and functioning of racially-mixed congregations in South Africa" in *Religion in a Changing World* edited by Madeleine Cousineau. Westport, CT: Greenwood Publishers, 1998.

Washington, Raleigh and Kehrein, Glen. *Breaking Down Walls: A model for reconciliation in an age of racial strife*. Chicago: Moody Press, 1993.

Welch, Sharon. "An Ethic of Solidarity and Difference" in *Postmodernism, Feminism and Cultural Politics: Redrawing Education Boundaries*, edited by Henry A. Giroux. Albany: State University of New York Press, 1991.

Yancey, George. One Body, *One Spirit: Principles of Successful Multiracial Churches*. Downers Grove: InterVarsity Press, 2003.

Zahniser, A.H.M. *Symbol and Ceremony: Making disciples across cultures*. Monrovia: MARC, 1997.

Printed in the United States
109303LV00003B/169-186/A